ISBN-13: 978-0-9988350-0-6 (Paperback)
ISBN-10: 0998835005 (Paperback)

ISBN-13: 978-0-9988350-1-3 (E-book)
ISBN-10: 0-9988350-1-3 (E-book)

Library of Congress Control Number: 2017904147

For more information visit:
www.GettingAdmitted.com

For more individualized assistance visit:
www.TheIvyCounselor.com

Countless high school students are using this guide and getting admitted to great colleges including Ivy League and other very selective colleges, to highly selective colleges with merit aid and to selective colleges with full-tuition scholarships. College admission results, however, are not guaranteed.

Every year it seems to get harder to get admitted to college. Application numbers keep going up (over 100,000 per year at UCLA), and acceptance rates keep going down (under 5% at Stanford). Thousands of perfect ACT/SAT/GPA scoring students, and hundreds-of-thousands of lower scoring applicants, regularly get rejected from universities that they thought would accept them.

Traditionally, a regional admissions officer would spend 12-15 minutes on your initial application review. Recently, however, many over-worked offices have revamped the process, with two cross-region admissions officers simultaneously reviewing each application for 4-6 minutes. So, you have approximately five minutes to wow the judges, and move on to the selections committee.

While you sit on one side of a scale, your competition sits on the other. The odds are stacked against you. What, if anything, can you do to tip the scale in your favor?

The answer is the same for every high school student and every college. And, it's not as hard as it seems. You just need access to the same "secrets" that college admissions experts are selling to their clients for hundreds of dollars an hour.

This step-by-step guide grants you that access. It reveals the 12 things that matter most in the admissions process, and provides corresponding steps for getting admitted. It's like having your own private college counselor right at your fingertips.

Every single paragraph contains important information that will help weigh your odds. Aim to complete each step within its target time period, beginning the summer before junior year and ending the summer before senior year. If the date has already passed, complete the step as soon as possible.

After you have checked off each step, your applications will be complete. You will then be able to relax and enjoy senior year. But, don't relax and enjoy it too much, because colleges can, and do, rescind acceptances.

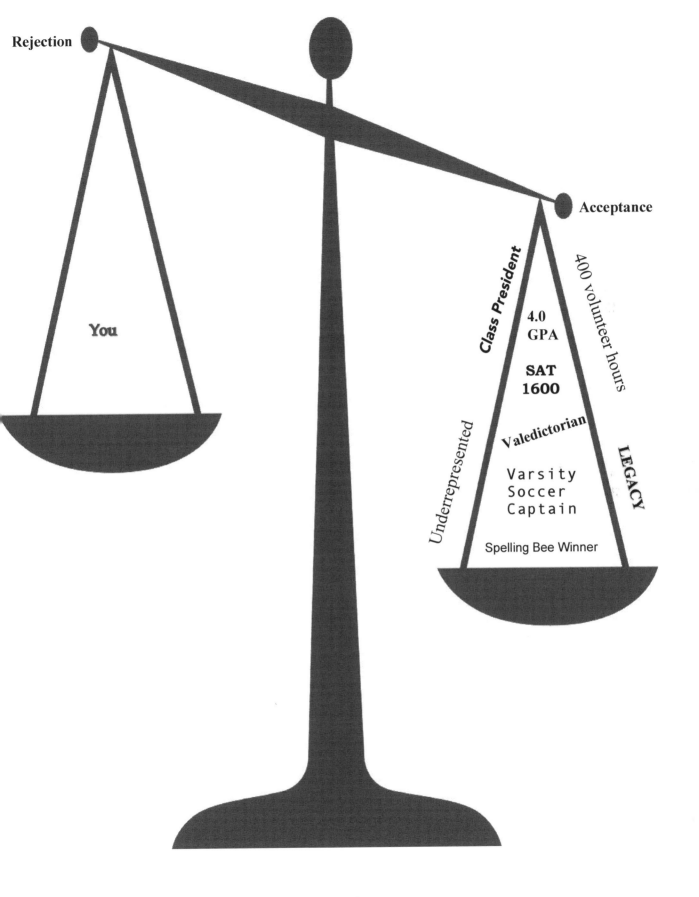

Rejection

Acceptance

You

Class President

4.0 GPA

SAT 1600

400 volunteer hours

Underrepresented

Valedictorian

LEGACY

Varsity Soccer Captain

Spelling Bee Winner

Table of Contents

I. STANDING OUT FROM THE CROWD MATTERS......................................6

    (Target Date: Summer Before Junior Year)

    Step 1 Checklist..11

II. STANDARDIZED TEST SCORES MATTER 16

    (Target Date: Summer Before Junior Year - June of Junior Year)

    Step 2 Checklist..27

III. COUNSELOR & TEACHER RECOMMENDATIONS MATTER.....................28

    (Target Date: September - June of Junior Year)

    Step 3 Checklist..34

IV. GRADES MATTER...35

    (Target Date: September - June of Junior Year)

    Step 4 Checklist..38

V. FIT MATTERS...39

    (Target Date: December of Junior Year)

    Step 5 Checklist..51

VI. CHANCES MATTER..52

    (Target Date: January of Junior Year)

    Step 6 Checklist..60

VII. YIELD MATTERS..61

    (Target Date: February of Junior Year - Acceptance)

    Step 7 Checklist..66

VIII. IMAGE MATTERS...**67**

    (Target Date: March of Junior Year)

    Step 8 Checklist...**70**

IX. THE RATIO OF APPLICATIONS MATTERS...**71**

    (Target Date: April of Junior Year)

    Step 9 Checklist...**74**

X. TIMING MATTERS...**75**

    (Target Date: May of Junior Year)

    Step 10 Checklist...**79**

XI. ESSAYS AND SHORT ANSWERS MATTER...**80**

    (Target Date: Summer Before Senior Year)

    Step 11 Checklist...**88**

XII. APPLICATION DETAILS MATTER...**89**

    (Target Date: Summer Before Senior Year)

    Step 12 Checklist...**91**

APPENDICES:

1. Important Things To Do After Applying...**92**

2. Sample Spreadsheet...**102**

I

Standing Out From the Crowd Matters

STEP 1 – MAKE A LIST OF YOUR STANDOUT TRAITS AND ACCOMPLISHMENTS

(Target Date: Summer Before Junior year)

Colleges seek to build a class of accomplished students. In order to tip the scale in your favor, you need to stand out from thousands of other applicants. Good grades and scores alone are not enough to get you admitted to selective schools.

A. Make a list of your traits and accomplishments.

Your list should include: sport, club and community service involvement; academic achievements; activities outside of school including hobbies, summer jobs, interesting trips, and college classes. You never know what might catch an admission officer's eye.

Keep in mind that colleges will likely compare your application to others from your own high school. If you attend a high achieving high school with many impressive students applying to the same colleges, you will need even greater attributes to stand out amongst your classmates.

B. Underline all <u>extra traits/accomplishments</u> that help you stand out even better.

Underline all of your extra traits/accomplishments, which include any unique talents/traits, leadership positions, sustained interest in activities, legacy and diversity.

1. Unique Talents/Traits

Unique talents and traits make you stand out from the crowd. If you are a juggler who performs in a traveling summer circus, or a person who can solve the Rubik's Cube while blindfolded, these things could help make you memorable to admissions officers. Other traits, such as a "first-generation" status (first generation in your family to attend college) can also help weigh odds in your favor.

2. Leadership Positions

The better you demonstrate your ability to lead, the better your chances of admission. While anyone can join the Robotics Club, only one person can be the Founder or President of the Robotics Club. If you have not been appointed or elected to any significant positions, do not be afraid to create your own.

Leadership comes in many shapes and forms. For example, if you are too busy helping out at home to join clubs or play sports, you can demonstrate leadership by describing your family responsibilities. Things like baby-sitting your siblings, and making dinner for your family on weekday nights, count.

3. Sustained Interest

College applications are filled with questions about prospective students' passions. Passions are things that you enjoy so much that you do them every chance you get. Sustained interest in an activity therefore demonstrates your passion for it.

Even better than everyday passions are unique passions. Thousands of applicants are passionate about sports but less are passionate about saving endangered gorillas. The more unique your passion, the more you will stand out.

Make your passion memorable in your applications by pursuing your interest even further than other students. For example, if you love to run, organize an annual race to benefit a local charity. If you are an obsessive bargain hunter, start a weekly blog about your amazing finds.

4. Legacy

Legacy students are the children, or other close relatives, of a graduate of the college. Some schools place a lot of importance on legacy. Others do not factor it in at all.

5. Diversity

Diversity can come from many areas, including race, nationality, religion, and even place of residence. Whatever differences you possess, put them on your list now so that you don't forget to make them known in your applications.

C. Bold or highlight all extraordinary traits/accomplishments that make you stand out best.

Extraordinary traits/accomplishments are often considered to be "hooks" that help students get accepted into the most selective colleges. Hooks include nationally recognized achievements, special talents, and certain minority, legacy and social status. Most students do not have any hooks, but if you do, bold or highlight them.

1. Nationally Recognized Achievements

Nationally recognized achievements are those that only few have achieved. For example, only one student wins the Intel Science Award every year, and only two from every state are named Presidential Scholars. These types of accomplishments are rare, and really make you stand out from the crowd.

2. Special Talents

Special talents are those that only a small amount of applicants possess. For example, only a fraction of students are nationally ranked athletes or award-winning professional actors. The more special your talent, the more that colleges will want to accept you.

3. Certain Minority Status

Certain groups such as Native Americans, Hispanics, Mexicans and African Americans are under-represented at many colleges. If you belong to one of those groups, it could help you get admitted to one of those schools.

4. Certain Legacy Status

At most schools, being a legacy alone is not a hook. However, the child of a major legacy contributor might have a hook.

5. Certain Social Status

Some colleges are impressed with certain social statuses. For example, children of well-known businesspeople, politicians or celebrities could have a hook.

D. Research The Common Data Set to determine the importance placed on numerous academic and non-academic factors in admissions.

The Common Data Set (CDS) initiative is a collaborative effort among data providers in the higher education community and publishers as represented by the College Board, Peterson's, and U.S. News & World Report. You can research specific schools to determine if they report CDS information by searching the Internet for the college name and "Common Data Set." Unfortunately, not all colleges report this data.

If a college does report the data, section C7 lists the relative importance of the following academic and non-academic factors in freshman admissions as "very important," "important," "considered," and "not considered":

Academic
Rigor of secondary school record
Class rank
Academic GPA
Standardized test scores
Application Essay
Recommendation

Non-academic
Interview
Extracurricular activities
Talent/ability
Character/personal qualities
First generation
Alumni/ae relation
Geographical residence
State residency
Religious affiliation/commitment
Racial/ethnic status
Volunteer work
Work experience
Level of applicant's interest

http://www.commondataset.org/docs/2016-2017/CDS_2016-2017.htm

Examples of the different levels of accomplishment/traits:

Academics:

Honor Society Member (Accomplishment)
<u>*Honor Society Vice President*</u> *(Extra Accomplishment)*
National Presidential Scholar *(Extraordinary Accomplishment)*

Top 10% Rank (Accomplishment)
<u>*Valedictorian*</u> *(Extra Accomplishment)*
National Spelling Bee Winner *(Extraordinary Accomplishment)*

Science Olympiad Team Member (Accomplishment)
<u>*Science Olympiad State Competition Winner*</u> *(Extra Accomplishment)*
U.S. Intel Science Winner *(Extraordinary Accomplishment)*

Took IB Level Classes (Accomplishment)
<u>*Received IB Diploma*</u> *(Extra Accomplishment)*
Received Nobel Prize *(Extraordinary Accomplishment)*

Other:

Varsity Athlete (Accomplishment)
<u>*4 year Varsity Athlete; Co-Captain*</u> *(Extra Accomplishment)*
Nationally Ranked Athlete *(Extraordinary Accomplishment)*

Drama Club Member (Accomplishment)
<u>*Drama Club Founder*</u> *(Extra Accomplishment)*
Emmy-nominated Actor *(Extraordinary Accomplishment)*

Legacy (Trait)
<u>*Large Donor Legacy*</u> *(Extra Trait)*
College Building Named After Parent *(Extraordinary Trait)*

Fast food Full-time Summer Drive-thru Attendant (Accomplishment)
<u>*Retail Full-time Summer Manager*</u> *(Extra Accomplishment)*
Franchise Creator *(Extraordinary Accomplishment)*

STEP 1 CHECKLIST

MAKE A LIST OF YOUR STANDOUT TRAITS AND ACCOMPLISHMENTS

o Make a list of your traits and accomplishments

o Underline all <u>extra traits/accomplishments</u>, which includes unique talents/traits, leadership roles, sustained interest, legacy and diversity

o **Bold** or highlight all extraordinary traits/accomplishments, which includes nationally recognized achievements, special talents, and certain statuses

o Research The Common Data Set to determine the importance placed on numerous academic and non-academic factors in admissions

FRESHMAN YEAR:
Sports

Clubs

Community service

Academic achievements

Hobbies

Summer jobs

Interesting trips

College summer classes

Other

SOPHOMORE YEAR:
Sports

Clubs

Community service

Academic achievements

Hobbies

Summer jobs

Interesting trips

College summer classes

Other

JUNIOR YEAR:
Sports

Clubs

Community service

Academic achievements

Hobbies

Summer jobs

Interesting trips

College summer classes

Other

SENIOR YEAR:
Sports

ty service

Academic achievements

Hobbies

Summer jobs

Interesting trips

College summer classes

Other

Standardized Test Scores Matter

STEP 2– ACHIEVE YOUR BEST POSSIBLE TEST SCORES

(Target Date: Summer Before Junior Year - June of Junior Year)

Colleges like to admit students whose test scores raise their accepted and admitted averages. It is important to find out which test is best for you, and achieve your best scores. The best test for your friend or sibling might not be the best test for you.

Some colleges also require SAT II subject tests, so check requirements carefully.

A. Gather information about the tests from the official ACT and SAT websites, and understand the differences between them.

Information about the tests can be found can on the College Board and ACT websites.

The ACT site compares the tests here:

www.act.org/solutions/college-career-readiness/compare-act-sat/

and the test scores here:

http://www.act.org/content/dam/act/unsecured/documents/ACTCollegeBoardJointStatement.pdf

The SAT site compares the tests here:

https://collegereadiness.collegeboard.org/sat/inside-the-test/compare-new-sat-act

and the scores in Table 7 here:

https://collegereadiness.collegeboard.org/pdf/higher-ed-brief-sat-concordance.pdf

Additionally, score conversion charts can give you an estimate of how your score converts to a score on the other test. For example:

http://convertyourscore.org

B. Find out if you are eligible for test accommodations.

If you have an IEP or a 504 in high school, you will likely be automatically eligible for the same SAT accommodations, such as extra time. You can also apply for these accommodations with the ACT. A decision from the ACT can take up to 8 weeks (or even longer if you need to appeal), so check with your guidance office ASAP.

SAT accommodations:

https://www.collegeboard.org/students-with-disabilities/typical-accommodations/time

ACT accommodations:

http://www.act.org/content/act/en/products-and-services/the-act/accommodations.html

C. Take practice tests.

Take at least one full-length, timed official practice exam for both tests to help you decide which one you prefer. The official ACT and SAT test books contain practice tests. You can also find free official practice problems and tests on the Internet.

ACT practice problems:

http://www.act.org/content/act/en/products-and-services/the-act/test-preparation.html

SAT practice tests:

https://collegereadiness.collegeboard.org/sat/practice/full-length-practice-tests

Note that the PLAN and the PSAT taken in school during high school junior year are not comparable to full practice ACT/SATs, but that the PSAT will determine your National Merit status. A high score could help you receive admissions and scholarships, so it is important to be prepared for it on test day.

Scores required for National Merit Status by state:

D. Pick a test and try to stick with it.

After you have taken at least one full-length, timed official practice exam of each test, compare your results. Did you score considerably better on one over the other, or just find one easier to take? Pick the one that you prefer and try to stick with it.

E. Study for the test.

The summer before your junior year is a great time to start studying for the ACT or SAT. If you cannot study during the summer, study during junior year. Long weekends and school breaks are a good time to study.

1. Take more practice tests.

Plan to take a minimum of three full-length practice tests before taking the official test. Pencil in at least three blocks of five hours. If you can't fit in full-length, timed tests, schedule at least fifteen hour-long sessions of individual practice test sections.

2. Read prep books.

Although some students study solely by taking practice exams, others choose to also read prep books, such as the "official" ACT and SAT study books. There are also other options available from different publishers. Read reviews and browse library and bookstore shelves to determine which might work for you.

3. Consider taking a prep course and/or hiring a tutor.

If you are not scoring as well as you had expected, you might benefit from a prep course. Some high schools offer review classes as a part of their curriculum or host "boot camps" the weekend prior to the test. If your high school does not offer any options, search for other web-based or local test prep courses.

If money is not an issue, consider hiring a private tutor. Sometimes the difference between acceptance and rejection, or a scholarship, is just a few points. It might be well worth the cost and effort to try to raise your score.

F. Register for test dates.

Both tests have registration deadlines. Do not wait until the last minute to register for the tests. Some test centers fill up well before the deadline date.

1. Create an account on the official test website.

When you register, there will likely be a box to check if you wish to allow the ACT or SAT to release your profile information, including your GPA, to colleges. Be aware that colleges will not only use this info to determine if they want to admit you, but that they will also use it to determine if they do not want to admit you. It might not be in your best interest to check that box.

ACT:

http://www.act.org/content/act/en/products-and-services/the-act.html

SAT:

https://cbaccount.collegeboard.org/iamweb/smartRegister?appId=292&DURL=https%3A%2F%2Faccount.collegeboard.org%2Fprofessional%2Fdashboard

2. Decide on whether to take the writing section.

Both tests offer a writing section. Some colleges require it, while others do not. To keep your options open, take the writing section of the test at least once.

3. Decide on how many times to take the test.

Plan to take either test at least twice. Sometimes, test dates or scores get cancelled for unforeseen reasons, like bad weather or suspected cheating in the test room. If you wait until your senior year to take either test for the first time, and you get sick or a storm cancels the test, you could end up in a bad situation.

Also, many colleges "super-score" the SAT, and some do the same for the ACT. This means that colleges will accept the highest score from each individual section, not just every test date. So, if you re-take the exam and your score goes up in one section but down in the others, it will help you, not hurt you.

SAT score-use practices by different colleges:

https://securemedia.collegeboard.org/digitalServices/pdf/professionals/sat-score-use-practices-participating-institutions.pdf

Keep in mind that while most colleges suggest that you not take any exam more than three times, some offer automatic merit awards for certain scores. If you only need only one ACT point or 50 SAT points to qualify for a scholarship, it might be worth it to take the test again. You can wait until after you have applied/been accepted, as long scores can still be submitted before the deadline.

4. Decide on when to take the test(s).

Most students take standardized tests during their junior year of high school. Some start even earlier. However, never take an official test to practice, since many colleges require that you report every score taken of a test while attending high school.

Some students speculate that certain months are better than others to take the tests, because they believe that curve will be easier at those times. There is no evidence to suggest that this theory is true. More significant than any particular date, is to be sure that on the date, you feel well and well-prepared.

Leave yourself enough time to take the test at least twice, and also any required subject tests, before applications are due. A great plan is to have all of your tests completed before senior year, so that you can devote that summer to your applications.

For example, take the SAT in August and October of junior year. If after scores are released, it is necessary to try the other test, register for the February and April ACTs. Or, take the ACTs in September and October and then the SAT in January and March, if necessary.

ACT test dates:

http://www.act.org/content/act/en/products-and-services/the-act/registration.html

SAT Test dates:

https://collegereadiness.collegeboard.org/sat/register/dates-deadlines

5. Decide on where to take the test(s).

The tests are offered in different places, and not always at your own high school. Choose a convenient location. You don't want to wake up on test day and realize that your test center is 100 miles away.

ACT test centers:

http://www.act.org/content/act/en/products-and-services/the-act/registration/test-center-locator.html

SAT test centers:

https://collegereadiness.collegeboard.org/sat/register/find-test-centers

6. Pay for the test date(s).

Don't forget to submit payment while registering for a test date. Information about test fee waivers can be found online.

ACT fee waivers:

https://www.act.org/content/dam/act/unsecured/documents/FeeWaiver.pdf

SAT fee waivers:

https://collegereadiness.collegeboard.org/sat/register/fees/fee-waivers

7. Keep a copy of your registration confirmation(s).

Screenshot and/or print out your registration confirmation page for your records.

8. Decide on how many free score reports you will send.

Both tests allow you to choose some free score reports to colleges of your choice. The downside is that you must choose the schools before you actually receive your scores. This could result in your most selective colleges receiving scores that you would rather they didn't see.

If you don't want to "waste" the free reports, it is a good idea to only send them to the colleges on your list with the lowest average accepted and admitted test scores.

ACT score policies:

http://www.act.org/content/act/en/products-and-services/the-act/scores.html

SAT score policies:

https://collegereadiness.collegeboard.org/sat/scores

G. Prepare for test day.

Before you take the test, make sure that you are completely prepared for test day.

1. Follow online instructions.

Know what is required and allowed (pencils, certain calculators, snacks, etc.) and what is not allowed (cell phones, scrap paper, etc.) in the test center.

ACT test procedures:

http://www.act.org/content/act/en/products-and-services/the-act/test-day.html

SAT test procedures:

https://collegereadiness.collegeboard.org/sat/taking-the-test/what-to-expect

2. Print out your test ticket.

You will need to bring your test ticket with you with you to the test. If you misplace it, you can re-print it from your online ACT or SAT account.

3. Have photo ID ready.

You will be required to show your school ID, driver's license or passport as follows:

ACT test day requirements:

http://www.act.org/content/act/en/products-and-services/the-act/test-day.html

SAT test ID requirements:

4. Know exactly where you will be going and how to get there.

Confirm the test center location, double check its address and determine how long it will take for you to get there with traffic.

H. Take the test, but only if you are feeling well and well-prepared that day.

If you are not feeling your best on test day, re-schedule. There might be a fee to do so, but it will be well worth it since you will never achieve your best scores when you are feeling under the weather. Login to your account as soon as possible to make changes to your registration.

I. Review after-test options.

If you do not do as well as expected, consider options available to you.

ACT:

1. Cancel your ACT score.

If you wish to cancel your ACT score, you must make that request to your proctor on the date of the test, before you leave the test center. Remember that test scores are curved, so just because it seemed particularly hard does not necessarily mean that you won't do as well as on practice tests. Also, since you can delete a test record after receiving your score, this option should at most times be avoided.

http://www.act.org/content/act/en/products-and-services/the-act/scores.html

2. Cancel free ACT score reports.

You can edit/cancel your free ACT score reports on the ACT website up to the Thursday after a Saturday test. To do so, login to your ACT account, and change or delete your choices.

3. Order a copy of your ACT test questions and answers.

The ACT website states that you have up to three months after the most U.S. ACT test dates to verify your scores. See below:

You will receive a copy of the multiple-choice test questions used to determine your score, a list of your answers, and the answer key. (If you t took the writing test, you will also receive a copy of the writing prompt, the scoring rubric, and the scores assigned to your essay by two readers.) Information about ordering a photocopy of your answer document (including your essay if you took the writing test) for an additional fee will be included with your materials.

http://www.act.org/content/act/en/products-and-services/the-act/your-scores/request-a-copy.html

4. Request corrections of any ACT errors.

If you find errors after verifying your scores, you can ask that they be corrected within three months of receiving your score report. You can also request hand scoring for an additional fee. Scores might go up, but will not go down.

https://www.act.org/content/act/en/products-and-services/the-act/your-scores/score-reports.html

5. Delete the ACT test record.

If, before you send score reports for certain dates, you wish to delete those scores from your ACT record so that they are no longer available to be sent to colleges who request "all scores," you can send a letter to the ACT making that request:

Students own their test scores and may direct ACT to delete their scores for a particular test date from our records. (Note: Students may not delete scores used to document participation in State and District Testing.)

To delete your scores for a particular test date, you must submit a written request. Provide us with your name and home address, and we will mail you a form to complete and return to us. We will then permanently r remove your record for that test date from our files. All scores from that test date will be deleted.
Write to:
ACT Institutional Services
P.O. Box 168
Iowa City, IA 52243-0168

http://www.act.org/content/act/en/products-and-services/the-act/help.html

SAT:

1. Cancel your SAT score.

If you feel that you didn't do your best on the SAT, you can cancel your scores on the date of testing by completing a "request to cancel scores form" and returning it to the testing supervisor before leaving the test center, or up to 11:59 p.m. on the Wednesday after the test date via written and signed letter to the College Board. (Students with disabilities have until Monday one week after the published test date to cancel their scores, due to the extended school-testing window.)

Once a request to cancel scores has been submitted, scores cannot be reinstated or reported to you or any institutions.

https://collegereadiness.collegeboard.org/sat/scores/canceling-scores

2. Cancel free SAT score reports.

You can edit/cancel your free SAT score reports on the College Board website up to 9 days after the test. To do so, login to your account and change or delete your choices.

3. Order a copy of your SAT test questions and answers.

According to the College Board, tests taken on certain dates are eligible, for a fee, for Question and Answer or Student Answer services:

The Question-and-Answer Service (QAS) is a test-disclosure service that includes a booklet copy of the test you took with a table of correct answers and scoring information. You also receive a report that lists the type and level of difficulty of each question, along with what your answer was, and whether it was correct, incorrect, or omitted. The Student Answer Service (SAS) provides a report with information about the type of questions on your test, their level of difficulty, and whether your answers were correct, incorrect, or omitted.

You can use this information to determine if you made an obvious bubbling error or if your essay did not scan properly.

https://collegereadiness.collegeboard.org/sat/scores/verifying-scores

4. Request to have your SAT hand-scored.

For an additional fee, the College Board will hand-score your SAT and fix any bubbling or scanning errors. They service does not include re-reading an essay or appealing an essay score, or correcting bubbles that do not meet SAT guidelines such as incomplete markings. Unlike the ACT, while your score might go up after hand scoring, it also might go down. Proceed with caution!

https://collegereadiness.collegeboard.org/pdf/sat-score-verification-request-form.pdf

J. Try the other test, if necessary.

If after two attempts, your test scores do not match up with your expectations, and you still have enough time, take a full-length timed practice of the other test. If your comparable score on this test is significantly better than the other, it might be worth it to schedule and take this exam. Most colleges only expect you to report the scores from one test even if you take both.

K. Consider test-optional colleges, if necessary.

After completing all testing, you feel that your scores are inconsistent with your GPA, consider applying to some test-optional colleges. Many colleges do not require standardized test scores for admittance, however scholarships might still require them:

http://www.fairtest.org/university/optional

L. Take subject tests, if necessary.

Some colleges require, or strongly recommend, SAT II subject test for admission. Other times, students submit subject test scores to enhance their applications. If you will take any subject tests, remember to fit them into your timeline.

The best time to take a subject test is directly following the completion of its corresponding course. If you take physics during your junior year, schedule the physics subject test during June of that year, since the May date might conflict with any AP studying/testing. You can take more than one subject test on one date, but limit yourself to two, in order to be able do your best.

STEP 2 CHECKLIST

ACHIEVE YOUR BEST POSSIBLE TEST SCORES

o Gather information about the tests from the official ACT and SAT websites and understand the differences between them

o Find out if you are eligible for test accommodations

o Take practice tests

o Pick a test and try to stick with it

o Study for the test

o Register for test dates

o Prepare for test day

o Take the test

o Review after-test options

o Try the other test, if necessary

o Consider test-optional colleges, if necessary

o Take subject tests, if necessary

III

Counselor and Teacher Recommendations Matter

STEP 3 - GET TO KNOW YOUR GUIDANCE COUNSELOR AND TEACHERS

(Target Date: September - June of Junior Year)

Colleges seek to admit highly recommended students. Lower-ranked students with outstanding recommendations are sometimes admitted over higher-ranking students without memorable references. It is therefore never too early to make connections with your guidance counselor and teachers.

Guidance Counselors:

Colleges will ask your counselor about how the rigor of your schedule, your grades and your accomplishments compare to those of your classmates.

The Common App and the lesser-used Universal Application both utilize a "School Report" that asks for general student evaluations and how enthusiastically the counselor generally recommends the student for college admission. The Universal Application's report can be viewed here:

https://www.universalcollegeapp.com/documents/uca-school-report.pdf

The Common App also allows counselors to upload a Counselor Recommendation, where the counselor may provide answers to the following prompts:

- The duration and context in which you've known the applicant (short response)

- The first words that come to mind to describe the applicant (short response)

- A broad-based assessment addressing topics like academic and personal characteristics, contextual comments for the applicant's performance and involvement, and/or observed problematic behaviors that an admissions committee should explore further (long response)

A. Make an appointment to meet with your guidance counselor no later than

fall of your junior year.

Try to meet with your Guidance Counselor at least once per high school year. In the very least, meet in the early fall of your junior year. If that time has already passed, then plan meet as soon as possible.

B. Review Your Transcript.

It is important to review your transcript, check for errors, and that you are on track to graduate on time. Some high schools report standardized test scores, absences and disciplines on transcripts. If you prefer that colleges not be sent certain information, ask if it can be removed from your transcript.

C. Ask for advice, even if you think that you don't need it.

In many cases, your guidance counselor is your direct link to admissions officers, so strive to make a good impression. Ask specific questions about selecting recommenders and colleges. And, since colleges will ask your counselor about the rigor of your coursework compared to your classmates, ask what classes you need to select in order for your schedule to be considered "most" or "very rigorous."

D. Give your guidance counselor information about you that s/he can use in your college reports.

Provide information about you to your guidance counselor even if s/he does not ask for it. S/he may not be aware of all of your achievements, so include items from your Step 1 list that can be used in the School Report.

Some counselors request information from parents. For example, your counselor might ask your parent to write a note about what makes them proud of you. Make sure that your parent submits a thoughtful response by the date requested.

E. Waive your right to read letters of recommendation.

Many teachers and counselors will not write letters unless a student waives the right to read them. Also, colleges like to know that you did not expect to read your letters of recommendations, so that writers can be candid and truthful. It is therefore in your best interest to sign a FERPA release waiving your right to read letters of recommendation:

http://www.ed.gov/policy/gen/guid/fpco/ferpa/index.html

F. Add your guidance counselor's name and proper contact information to your Naviance account and all applications, as required.

You will be asked add your counselor's name and email address to Naviance, the Common App, and other applications. Sometimes, counselors use a separate email address for this purpose. Use correct spelling and contact information.

G. Take counselor advice with a grain of salt.

Most counselors are very knowledgeable, but none can know everything about all colleges, or about you. Many students who have been told that they would "never" or would "definitely" get accepted to a college have been shocked with their admission decision. If you feel strongly about a school one way or the other, follow you gut.

Teachers:

Expect to submit at least one teacher letter of recommendation from an academic subject taught during your junior year. While some colleges do not require or accept recommendations, many will ask for two from different academic subjects. Others also accept letters from a parent, peer, boss or coach. Check specific details carefully.

A. Determine which teachers might write you the best recommendations.

References will not address grades alone, so do not automatically ask for letters from teachers who awarded you the highest scores. A mediocre recommendation from a class where you received an "A+" will not be as memorable as a stellar letter from a "B+" class. When deciding on which teacher to ask, focus on who knows you and likes you best.

Think about the classes where you were most eager to learn and willing to participate. If you intend to major in Math, it might seem wise to ask your junior year math teacher. There might be a better choice, though, if you have not formed any connection with that teacher. Someone who has also served as your coach or club advisor could be the best choice.

B. Request letters of recommendation before the end of junior year.

Do not wait until your senior year to ask for recommendations. Some teachers limit how many they will write. Spring of your junior year is usually a good time to ask.

1. Ask for letters of recommendation in person.

Do not text or email to ask for a letter of recommendation. If the teacher has office hours, visit during that time, or schedule an appointment to make the request. During the meeting, let the teacher know why you have enjoyed the class, and then ask if s/he would be willing to write you a letter of recommendation.

For example: "Ms. Smith, I really enjoyed our circle talks every morning and your assignments have really helped me to become a better writer. As a result, I am now looking for colleges with strong journalism programs. I would really appreciate if you would be willing to write a letter of recommendation for me. I know that you are busy. Can you fit me in?"

2. Provide the teacher with self-addressed/stamped envelopes as required.

If a letter must be mailed to a college, provide the recommender with everything that s/he will need to easily get it there. If you cannot print out the envelope, write neatly.

3. Only ask for as many recommendations as you need.

Some students ask for more recommendations than they need, hoping to pick and choose from them at a later date. This is not a good idea, and doing so usually results in a fail. Teachers talk to each other, and can easily determine if you are talking advantage of their generosity.

C. Follow up with an emailed thank-you note.

As soon as possible after a teacher agrees to write a recommendation, email a thank-you note. Within the note, provide the teacher with pertinent information, and an "out" if s/he cannot follow through with the promised recommendation.

1. Provide the teacher with pertinent information about you, even if they didn't ask for it.

Include the following:

a. Your name

Do not only use your nickname. Include the exact spelling of your birth certificate name, which matches the name that you will be using on your application.

b. The specific colleges to which you expect to apply, if known

If your teacher is a graduate of one of the colleges, it might help boost your chances.

c. Your area of interest, if known

Your recommender might want to craft the letter based on your potential course of study.

d. A list of your accomplishments/traits

Your teacher may not be aware of all of your achievements. Don't be afraid to include a list of things from Step 1 that can be used in the letter.

2. Provide the teacher with the date that you require the letter, and an "out" if you believe that s/he cannot write a great recommendation for you by that date.

Let the teacher know that you will be submitting all of your applications early in the fall, and request that their letter be completed by October 1st. This will give you time, even for the earliest college deadlines, to secure a different recommendation if it becomes necessary.

If you suspect that the teacher has any hesitation about writing the letter, or will not be able submit it by that due date, also give the teacher the opportunity to opt out. For example:

"I know that you are very busy, so if there is any reason why you will not be able to finish the letter by October 1st, please let me know as soon as possible so that I can plan accordingly. "

D. Add recommenders' names and contact information to Naviance and applications, as required.

Once you have confirmed who will write your letters, add their names to sites such as Naviance and the Common Application. Some teachers use a separate email address for this purpose. Use correct spelling and contact information.

E. Attach letters of recommendation to your applications.

Determine how to properly attach letters of recommendation to your applications. Some need to be uploaded directly to the Common App while other colleges require that a recommender seal an envelope, sign over the seal, and send it via snail mail. Follow all directions meticulously.

Also, only attach the intended recommendation for each college. For example, if you have two teachers added to your Common App account, but a specific application only accepts one recommendation, attach the preferred recommendation to the application.

F. Check the status of your recommendations.

Check the status of your recommendations on the Common App site. Some colleges also allow you to check the completion of your application on their websites. Keep track of what you are missing, if anything.

G. Follow-up with teachers as necessary.

If a college has not received a recommendation by the date that you requested, contact the recommender. For example: "Ms. Smith, I wanted to let you know that the Common App has not received your letter of recommendation and that my application otherwise complete. Please let me know if you will not be able to submit the letter this week. Thanks so much!"

If at any point you have reason to believe that a letter will not get completed on time, ask your guidance counselor for advice on what to do next. If it becomes necessary to ask another teacher, apologize for the short notice, and explain what happened, so that it does not seem like you waited until the last minute to make the request. Profusely thank the new recommender.

STEP 3 CHECKLIST

GET TO KNOW YOUR GUIDANCE COUNSELOR AND TEACHERS

Guidance Counselors:

o Meet with your guidance counselor no later than first semester of junior year

o Review your transcript

o Ask for advice, even if you think that you don't need it

o Give your guidance counselor information about you that s/he can use in your college reports

o Waive your right to read letters of recommendation

o Add your guidance counselor's name and contact information to your Naviance account and all applications, as required

o Take counselor advice with a grain of salt

Teachers:

o Determine which teachers will write you the best recommendations

o Request letters of recommendation before the end of your junior year

o Follow up with an emailed thank-you note

o Add recommenders' names and contact information to Naviance and applications as required

o Attach letters of recommendation to your applications

o Check the status of your recommendations

o Follow-up with teachers as necessary

IV

Grades Matter

STEP 4 – ACHIEVE UPWARD-TREDNING, COMPETITIVE GRADES IN THE MOST RIGOROUS CLASSES POSSIBLE

(Target Date: September - June of Junior Year)

Colleges strive to admit students whose' GPAs raise their accepted and admitted averages. In order to weigh the odds in your favor, take the most rigorous courses that allow you to maintain competitive grades and display an upward trend. The more selective the college, the greater the expectation of rigor.

A. Take the most rigorous courses possible to maintain competitive grades.

Many students believe that in order for their schedule to be considered "very rigorous," they must take every AP/IB or Honors class available to them. This is not necessarily true, and the practice can actually backfire. Generally, taking 3-5 AP classes is sufficient for most colleges.

If you are overwhelmed with too many AP classes and your GPA suffers as a result, you might fall short of a college's accepted average. Additionally, many merit scholarships are GPA-based. If you classes are too difficult to achieve minimum scholarship GPAs, you will shut yourself out of opportunities, no matter how many AP classes you have taken.

Regarding Honors level classes, it is impossible to predict if it will be more advantageous to score a 4.0 in Introductory Algebra or a 3.0 in Honors Algebra, since the answer might be different at different colleges. The more selective the college, the more important it will be that you excelled in higher-level courses. However, a "C" in an advanced class will likely hurt more than it will help, and a "D" or "F" will actually disqualify you from certain schools.

To be safe, plan to take the highest level of a course where you can maintain at least a "B" or higher.

1. Understand that many colleges re-calculate GPAs.

Different high schools use different GPA scale. Some weigh advanced classes, while other do not. Colleges therefore usually re-calculate GPAs to standardize them.

To do so, some colleges only count core classes, while others also factor in electives. Some weigh advanced classes more than regular classes, while others do not. Some drop freshman scores, but not all do.

Accordingly, it is virtually impossible to predict which class choices will net you the best results. Your GPA will look different to each college, depending on many factors. So, plan to always take the highest level of a course where you can maintain at least a "B" or higher.

2. Consider, if possible, the courses and grades of other applicants from your high school.

As previously discussed, the School Report specifically asks your counselor how your course rigor compares to that of your classmates. If applicants from your school have taken more rigorous courses and/or received better grades than you, your application could literally end up at the bottom of your high school's pile. It is therefore very important to take into consideration the competition from your own classmates.

If you cannot keep up with your competing classmates' course rigor and grades (and scores and accomplishments), do not apply to the same colleges as them. Ask your counselor for guidance with this as needed.

B. Work hard to display an upward trend in grades.

Colleges look at grade patterns. A downward trend from freshman to senior year suggests that you might not be ready to handle college level courses. An upward trend, on the other hand, indicates that you are ready for a challenge.

1. Don't worry too much about freshman year grades.

Some colleges do not heavily weigh freshman year grades, or factor them in at all. If you have had a rough start, do not despair. There is still hope!

2. Place an emphasis on junior year classes and grades.

Colleges will not have much, if any, of your senior grades to consider when reviewing your application, so they will likely focus most on your junior year. Make sure that your junior year classes and grades are the most rigorous and best that can they can be. Do not fill junior year with easy electives or study halls.

3. Don't slack off during senior year.

Most colleges require mid-year and final reports of your senior year courses and grades. Any indication that you are suffering from "senioritis" could negatively impact a pending application or even an offer of admission. Do not significantly slack off during your senior year, even if you have been accepted early.

Also, do not drop any class unless it is absolutely necessary. If you must change your schedule, be prepared to explain why. Colleges can, and do, rescind offers of acceptance for course drops.

STEP 4 CHECKLIST

STEP 4 – ACHIEVE UPWARD-TREDNING, COMPETITIVE GRADES IN THE MOST RIGOROUS CLASSES POSSIBLE

o   Take the Most Rigorous Courses Possible to Maintain Competitive Grades

o   Work hard to display an upward trend in grades

V

Fit Matters

STEP 5 – FIND COLLEGES THAT YOU LIKE, AND WHO LIKE YOU BACK

(Target Date: December of Junior Year)

Colleges hope to boost their retention rates by accepting students who are likely to stay past freshman year. It matters to them that you are a good fit for their school, as much is it matters to you that the school is a good fit for you. It is therefore important to take time to research and find schools where you will fit in best.

There are lots of ways to find out more about what colleges you might want to attend. Word of mouth is great, but remember that what worked for your cousin or neighbor might not work for you. There are lots of books on the subject, and the Internet is also a great resource. The Common Data Set for specific colleges is, once again, very informative. Other helpful sites include:

https://niche.com

http://unigo.com

http://collegedata.com

http://colleges.usnews.rankingsandreviews.com/bestcolleges/rankings/national-universities

https://bigfuture.collegeboard.org/college-search

http://www.collegeconfidential.com

Whatever you do, do not fall in love with a "dream school" or get caught up in finding "first," "second" and "third" choice colleges. There is no such thing as a "perfect" school for anyone. Each one has pros and cons. The important thing is to find a few affordable colleges that you would be happy to attend if admitted.

Also, do not base your decision on rankings alone. A student who applies to every Ivy League college has not properly researched them. Although they are all top ranked, they are very different from each other in terms of location, size and "feel."

A. Think about what majors interest you.

What do you want to study?

Although you will likely change your mind at least once before college graduation, it is a good idea to think about what majors interest you. Start with what classes you have enjoyed the most in high school, and what career path you might like to follow. The following sites can help:

https://www.mynextmove.org/explore/ip

https://bigfuture.collegeboard.org/explore-careers

1. Determine if a college offers majors that interest you.

Not every college offers every major. If you are interested in something less common like Marine Biology, you will need to research which colleges offer that major. If you want to study Business, and it is important to you that the college has a separate "Business School," look for that.

You can check out more info about majors at specific colleges, and the sizes and ranks of the programs on sites like these:

https://nces.ed.gov/collegenavigator/

https://bigfuture.collegeboard.org/college-search

http://www.collegedata.com/cs/search/college/college_search_tmpl.jhtml

http://www.shanghairanking.com/index.html

2. Determine if colleges are accredited, and also accredited in your intended area of study.

First, look for colleges that are accredited by the U.S. Department of Education. If the college is not so accredited, it cannot offer federal aid, and course credit likely cannot be transferred to an accredited institution:

https://ope.ed.gov/accreditation/Search.aspx

Next, look to see if your preferred major, like Journalism or Business, are voluntarily accredited by an agency like The Accrediting Council on

Education in Journalism and Mass Communications or the AACSB. Such accreditation may or may not impact your future employment in the field. If the major is not accredited, find out why, and how it could affect you:

http://www.acejmc.org

http://www.aacsb.edu/accreditation/accredited-members/global-listing

3. Find out how majors are declared.

Do some research to determine how majors are declared at specific colleges, and what your back up plan might be if your intended course of study does not work out.

Some schools ask you to indicate a major on their application, but your choice is not binding. These schools admit you to their general class, and ask you to declare, or apply for, a specific major at a later time. Your choice of a major on your application has less of an effect on your admissions chances than at colleges who accept students into specific majors.

Others colleges accept you specifically into the major that you selected on their application. This could force you to choose between two or more possible paths, a year before classes begin. This decision might also greatly affect your admissions chances, since some majors require higher stats than others.

4. Discover how difficult it is to change majors after acceptance or enrollment.

At some schools, changing majors is a breeze. At others, it is nearly impossible. It is better to think it through now than to be unpleasantly surprised at a later date.

5. Discover whether certain majors are "impacted."

At some colleges, certain majors have limited enrollment. At these schools, sophomore and junior students sometimes learn that their preferred major not available to them, despite impressive grades. If you will not be satisfied settling for a different major, it is best to avoid schools with impacted majors in your interest.

B. Decide on selectivity.

Are you impressed with selectivity?

Colleges are often classified as "Most Selective," "Very Selective," "Selective" or "Less Selective," depending their percentage of admitted students. The most selective schools have the lowest percentage of admitted students and often the highest prestige and rankings, but often offer little to no merit aid. Less selective schools, on the other hand, often offer enticing scholarships, and sometimes also amazing opportunities to succeed.

Many people believe that they should go to the best college on their list. But what does "best" mean? Is it necessarily the most selective school?

You need to think about not only where you will get the best education, but also where you will fit in the best and have the best overall experience. Although an Ivy league college might look great on your resume, it may not have as big of an impact as you think, and the cons might actually outweigh the pros. Ask yourself:

1. Do you want to be surrounded by students who are smarter than you, or would you like to rank closer to the top of your class?

2. Will competition for leadership positions, internships and clubs be too tough at a very selective college?

3. If you have plans to attend graduate school, will it be difficult to attain a strong enough GPA at a very selective college to do so? Some Graduate schools have GPA admissions minimums, for example, of 3.5 and up.

4. Are you hoping for merit aid? If so, colleges that are generally "beneath" your stats are the ones that will likely offer you the most money. It might be worth it to attend a less selective college at a reduced cost than a very selective college at full cost.

If you decide that a most selective college is for you, know that most of these colleges claim to have "holistic" admissions, which means that they consider the whole person and not just scores and grades. However, they still require highly impressive GPAs and test scores. Although >/=1500 SAT or 33 ACT and >/= 3.8 un-weighted GPA are widely regarded as the unwritten thresholds to admission for the most selective schools, these scores are by no means a guarantee of acceptance to any selective school.

If you decide instead that you prefer a less selective college, check out the list below. These are colleges that regularly accept "B" students, and may also offer scholarships to students with higher averages:

C. Look at size.

What size college/campus/classes are you leaning towards?

Size does matter. Some students look forward to mingling with 30,000 other classmates. Others would be rendered speechless in a lecture of 400.

Take a look not only at numbers of students and acres of land, but also the teacher/student ratio. Find out how many seats the largest lecture hall holds. Although big universities often offer big opportunities and a large alumni network, small colleges might be a better fit for many students.

The CDS reports Enrollment in questions B1 and B2, and Faculty and Class Size in I1 through I3.

D. Discover what types of colleges you prefer.

What type of college do you prefer?

There are lots of different types of colleges. The things that you are looking for might be better found at one over another. Determining what types of colleges you like best will help you narrow down your list.

1. "College" or "University?"

"Colleges," which tend to be smaller institutions, do not offer a full spectrum of graduate level courses or degrees and may not be accredited. Universities, on the other hand, offer full undergraduate and graduate level study, usually in at least several fields. If it is important for you to have access to accreditation and full graduate level programs on campus, then focus on "Universities," not "Colleges."

2. Public or Private?

Private schools often carry prestige, large endowments and even bigger tuition bills. Often, though, merit or need-based scholarships offset high prices. Sometimes, private schools can be a better bargain than your own state university.

Public colleges are sometimes associated with bigger classes, lower costs and party scenes. But, these are just generalizations that may or may not be correct. Many student find that a state school offers them everything that they want and need, and often at a very reasonable cost.

There are pros and cons to both. Compare them to see what is best for you. If a state is in financial crisis and you won't be able to get the classes that you need to graduate within four years, or caps out-of-state admission and financial aid, factor that into your decision. (The CDS reports Residency in the Student Life section F1.)

3. Liberal Arts or Technical?

Liberal Arts colleges do not strive to teach skills, but rather provide a broad education. Technical colleges focus on preparing students for the workforce. If you prefer one or the other, make note of it.

4. Division I, II or III?

NCAA Division I colleges recruit elite athletes and offer corresponding athletic scholarships and athletic programs. Division II and III colleges may also have impressive teams and spirit, but offer few to no athletic scholarships. If you cannot imagine yourself at a school without a team (and I don't mean a good team, I mean any team at all), look into the sports that are offered.

Do not assume that because there is a team, there are also fans on campus. If school spirit is important to you, find out if most students attend sporting events. And if you aspire to walk-on and play, look for available club teams in case you do not make the team.

5. Co-Ed or Single Gender?

If you don't think that you can survive without mingling with the opposite sex on a regular basis, it is probably best to opt co-ed. However, some single gender colleges partner with mixed colleges. It might be worth it to research further before you decide.

Also check out male to female ratios on campus. Many schools are close to 50%/50%, while others are farther apart. The CDS reports Admissions information in question C1.

6. Religious or Secular?

Many "Jesuit" and other religious-affiliated schools are not much different from secular colleges. Others require participation in religious classes and mass. If you would not feel comfortable in a particular situation, do not apply.

7. Score-Reliant or Test-Optional?

Some colleges do not require standardized scores from recent high school students. Others only exempt students who meet minimum GPAs or rankings. As previously noted, if there is a discrepancy between your GPA and your SAT/ACT scores, apply to some test-optional schools.

8. Semester or Trimester?

Colleges on a semester system offer two 15 or 16 week semesters, with winter and summer breaks in between. Student usually takes four or five classes per semester to graduate in four years.

Colleges on a trimester (also called a quarter) system have three 10-week trimesters, shorter vacations, and the option for an additional summer semester. Students usually take three classes per trimester to graduate in four years.

While some students enjoy the fast pace of a trimester system, others feel rushed. If you get bored quickly, trimesters might be for you. If you like to take your time with things, semesters could be the better choice.

9. Co-op or Traditional?

A college Co-op program offers work experience for a semester of each school year. Sometimes, students earn a salary, which is not counted towards FAFSA's family contribution. Some students are hired as full-time employees upon graduation.

While many students rave about Co-ops, others complain that the program fractures the college experience, even for the non-participating students on campus. For example, with students are constantly coming and going, it can be harder for friendships to be formed. If you are interested in, or concerned about Co-ops, find out if they are popular at the colleges that interest you.

10. Liberal or Conservative?

Many college campuses are very liberal. Some are more conservative. If you lean one way or the other, determine how the feel of a college might affect your comfort on campus.

E. Determine how much you can afford to spend on college.

Will you be able to afford a college if you get admitted?

Even schools with the lowest tuition bills can amount to tens of thousands of dollars each year. Sometimes room, board and fees add up to even more than tuition. Students who qualify for substantial financial aid often still leave college with massive debt. The CDS reports Annual Expenses in question G and Financial Aid In section H.

Now is the time to talk honestly with your family about what, if anything, they are willing or able to contribute to your costs. If you cannot afford a specific college, it is probably best to move on early. Most college websites provide a cost estimator web page that will ask you to plug in info and will then spit out an approximate amount of aid that you can expect if admitted. Keep the following in mind:

1. Student loans are usually restricted to $5500 per year.

2. Expenses such as books, travel, and incidentals can add thousands the equation.

3. Even if the FAFSA determines that you qualify for a certain amount of financial need-based aid, not all colleges agree to meet full financial need. Only certain colleges agree to meet your "full-need," as determined by the FAFSA, CSS, or their own calculations:

http://www.usnews.com/education/best-colleges/paying-for college/articles/2016-09-19/colleges-that-claim-to-meet-full-financial-need

4. Colleges that are not "need blind" often base admissions decisions on who will be able to pay full price without any aid. At these colleges, lower stat applicants who can pay-in-full may be accepted over higher stat applicants who require financial aid. Keep this in mind when applying and requesting financial aid at these schools.

5. Some colleges "front load" financial offers. This means that the package offered to freshman might be much higher than for subsequent years. Could you stay if that happened?

6. Merit-based scholarships are usually tied to your college GPA, which is not guaranteed. If your grades fall below the required level and you lose a

scholarship, would you be forced to drop out?

7. Colleges whose stats are "beneath" your stats are more likely to offer you merit aid. The higher your stats are over their averages, the more they might offer you.

F. Determine the locations that you prefer.

Do you want to be close to home or a plane trip away? Will you require a "College Town" with a coffee shop within walking distance? How important is safety?

Different locations offer differ experiences. While one person feels comfortable in the middle of a large city, another seeks a college bubble off the beaten path. A great college in the "wrong" location for you is not a good fit.

If safety is a big concern, it is important to search for crime stats to determine if you would feel safe at a particular college. Perform a search of the college name and the college town name and words like "crime," "murder," "sexual assault," "rape," "armed robbery" and "assault." If you are uncomfortable by the amount of hits that you receive, look elsewhere.

Also, even if you think that you want to be far from home, find at least one affordable close-to-home college to put on your list. Sometimes, plans change between application and enrollment.

G. Look into what kinds of housing are offered and/or required.

Where do you want to live?

Although housing need not be a game-changer, it can be for some students. Learn about what is available to students and then decide if it meets your needs. Do not expect to be able to pick your desired housing, especially as an underclassman.

Some colleges guarantee four years of on-campus housing while others have no guarantees at all. If you do not want to have to worry about moving off campus at some point, this information will be very important to you. Likewise, if a college requires that students live on campus freshman year or beyond, and you have no desire to do so, proceed with caution.

If you will only be comfortable if the college provides single-gender, LBGT, substance-free, honors, co-ed or gender-neutral dorms, ask if it is offered. Also, look at the different dorm offerings. Some are stuck in the '70s with cinderblock walls and limited Wi-Fi, housing six or more freshman together in converted lounges. Others are brand new suites with private bathrooms. Though colleges might not publish specific housing information on their websites, you can learn a lot by searching the Internet for college housing reviews. For example:

https://www.niche.com/colleges/rankings/best-college-dorms/

Also, research housing percentages. At some schools, almost 100% of students live on campus, while at others, only a very small percent remain on campus after freshman year. This can greatly affect the "feel" of the campus, so make note of these numbers if they are important to you.

And do not forget to check into the costs and locations of off-campus housing. In some cities like San Francisco and New York, rents are sky-high. If you are forced to move off-campus, will you be able to afford a nearby room?

H. Research what types of transportation are available.

How do you plan to get to and from home and to and from classes?

Some colleges allow freshman to bring cars while others do not provide parking for any grade level. Large Universities often offer free busing, while others recommend that you bring a bike. Some colleges are easily accessible to Greyhound, Amtrak or a local airport, while others offer few options - Uber and Lyft might not even be available. If this information is pertinent to your search, make note of the information that you find.

I. Look at colleges' minimum requirements for acceptance.

Will your final your transcript meet a college's minimum requirements?

Some colleges require or strongly suggest three or four years of a foreign language. Others require or strongly suggest SAT subject tests. If you do not meet a school's minimum requirements now, and are unlikely to meet them in the future, it is best to look elsewhere.

Note that some schools have unique requirements that, if not met, will prevent your application from even being considered. For example, the California UCs require that certain "a-g" classes be fulfilled with a minimum of a "C" grade. So, if you have not taken a yearlong art class and received a "C" or better, your application will be rejected.

J. Gather information about colleges' curriculums.

How much freedom do you want in your studies?

Some colleges offer flexible curriculums that allow students to study what they choose. Others have a rigid core curriculum that requires students to take years of pre-determined courses. Pay attention to curriculum requirements when researching colleges to add to your list.

K. Look at college retention rates.

How happy can you expect to be?

If a college has a high retention rate of freshman students, it is a good sign that most accepted student are not only capable of the rigor of the school, but also glad to be there. Lower retention rates can be an indicator that freshman are either unhappy or unable to pass their classes. Any score lower than 90% warrants some attention. The CDS reports Retention Rates in question B22.

L. Research college reputations.

Would it worry you to hear that a college is considered to be a "party" or "suitcase" school?

Some colleges are known for their parties more than their academics. Others are said to clear out on weekends. If you are not comfortable with the general reputation of a school, it could be reason to cross it off your list.

M. Learn about the presence of Greek Life on campuses.

Do you plan to rush a fraternity or a sorority, or do you prefer to steer clear of Greek life?

Some colleges have a large percentage of Greek members and encourage rush before freshman classes even begin. Others refuse to recognize Greek life at all. If this is a make or break for you, do your research now so that you are not unpleasantly surprised when you arrive.

N. Research four and six year graduation rates.

Do you hope to graduate in four years?

High graduation rates can be an indication that professors are skilled and students are supported. Low graduation rates can be evidence that registration for required classes is restricted. If you are worried about being forced to spend extra time or money, research graduation rates. The CDS reports Graduation Rates in questions B4 throu9gh B11. Also see:

http://collegeresults.org

O. Look at job placement rates.

Will you be employable after graduation?

It is not always easy to find information about a college's job placement rate. If you cannot find it, search the college's career services webpage. Even is the rate is not specifically mentioned, you will likely be able to determine how much career support is offered to students based on the depth of the page.

P. Find out what extracurriculars are offered, and how competitive/active they are.

What do plan to do when you are not in class?

The more selective a college, the tougher the competition will be for everything, including clubs.

Although a college may offer hundreds of clubs, many might be so competitive that most students can never participate. For example, a club sports team might be filled with graduate students who played Division 1 while undergrads.

A quick Internet search can reveal if a college really offers what want. If a club's social media page hasn't been updated in a long time, it might not be active. If an activity does have a current social media presence, follow it and ask other members the questions that you might have.

Q. Find out what AP/IB/SAT II credits are accepted.

How many credits can you expect to transfer?

Some colleges offer credit for a variety of AP/IB/SAT II subjects with specified scores. Others limit credit to only certain classes/higher scores. Sometimes, scores can only be used for placement purposes.

Different policies could mean the difference between a student graduating early/with a double major at one school, and receiving no benefit at another. If this will impact your decision about where to apply and attend, search college websites for detailed information about it.

STEP 5 CHECKLIST

FIND COLLEGES YOU LIKE, AND WHO LIKE YOU BACK

o Think about what majors interest you

o Decide on how selective you want your college to be

o Look at size

o Discover what types of colleges you prefer

o Determine how much you can afford to spend on college

o Determine what locations you prefer

o Look into what kinds of housing are offered and/or required

o Research what types of transportation are available

o Look at colleges' minimum requirements for acceptance

o Get information about colleges' curriculums

o Look at college retention rates

o Research college reputations

o Learn about the presence of Greek life on campuses

o Research four and six year graduation rates

o Look for job placement rates

o Determine what extracurriculars are offered

o Find out what AP/IB/SAT II credits are accepted

VI

Chances Matter

STEP 6 – DETERMINE YOUR CHANCES AT THE SCHOOLS THAT INTEREST YOU

(Target Date: January of Junior Year)

It doesn't matter how much you like a school if you have no chance of getting admitted. Take time to determine your chances of acceptance at schools that interest you. Once you understand your chances, you will be able to further refine your list of potential applications.

First, never assume that you will "definitely" get in to any college. Crazy things happen every year that leave students, parents and guidance counselors scratching their heads. Sometimes, admissions offices make mistakes. Other times, colleges protect their yield by rejecting students deemed to be over-qualified, because they do not believe that the student will actually enroll if admitted.

Also, don't expect that because a college sends you mail, or even offers to waive your application fee, that you will be accepted. Sometimes colleges recruit people to reject, just to make their school seem more selective than it actually is.

No one knows what admissions will do, including the admissions officers themselves, until they do it. Your best bet at narrowing down your chances is to look at the facts.

A. Use your high school's Naviance account and The Common Data Set to compare yourself to other applicants from your high school, and across the country.

Naviance:

Naviance is a service that many high schools use to provide information to their students and to coordinate their students' college applications. Once your guidance office provides you with a user name and password, you will be able to make an account and start using the site. If your high school does not subscribe to Naviance, you might be able to contact Naviance or other local high schools for a guest password.

1. Use Naviance to find out how many students from your high school regularly get accepted to specific colleges.

Naviance provides information about how many students have applied to specific colleges from your high school over the past few years, and how many were accepted, rejected and waitlisted. This information will give you a general idea of the acceptance rates at your high school. Hooks will not appear, so extraordinary applicants might skew the numbers.

2. Use Naviance to see the accepted GPA and standardized test scores from your high school at specific colleges.

If numerous students from your high school apply to the same college, and that college usually only accepts ta few students from your high school, the top-scoring applicants from your school generally have a better chance of acceptance than the students at the bottom of the pile. Look at the GPA and ACT/SAT scatter grams to see where your grades and scores fit in:

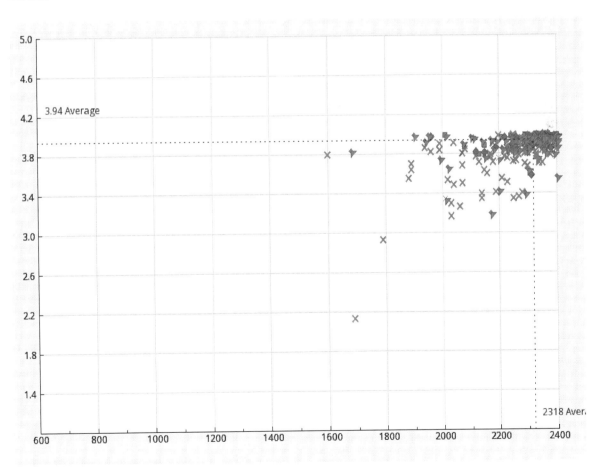

We've compared the scores of all the students who have been accepted from (your high school) with

your scores.
GPA
GOOD
You: 4
Average: 3.97
Lowest: 2.3 | Highest: 4

SAT
GOOD
You: 1550
Average: 1545
Lowest: 1210 | Highest: 1600

ACT
?
You: ?
Average: 33
Lowest: 30 | Highest: 36

OVERALL AVERAGE
GOOD
It looks like you are on track.

Common Data Set:

If a college reports Common Data Set information, use it to find the school's enrolled SAT/ACT and GPA ranges. The data will look like this:

http://www.commondataset.org/docs/2016-2017/CDS_2016-2017.htm

Freshman Profile:
Provide percentages for ALL enrolled, degree-seeking, full-time and part-time, first-time, first-year (freshman) students enrolled in Fall 2016, including students who began studies during summer, international students/nonresident aliens, and students admitted under special arrangements.

C9. Percent and number of first-time, first-year (freshman) students enrolled in Fall 2016 who submitted national standardized (SAT/ACT) test scores. Include information for ALL enrolled, degree-seeking, first-time, first-year (freshman) students who submitted test scores. Do not include partial test scores (e.g., mathematics scores but not critical reading for a category of students) or combine other standardized test results (such as TOEFL) in this item. Do not convert SAT scores to ACT scores and vice versa. Do convert New SAT scores (2016) to Old SAT scores using the College Board's concordance tools and tables (sat.org/concordance).

The 25th percentile is the score that 25 percent scored at or below; the 75th percentile score is the one that 25 percent scored at or above.

Percent submitting SAT scores _____   Number submitting SAT scores _____

Percent submitting ACT scores _____   Number submitting ACT scores _____

	25th Percentile	75th Percentile
SAT Critical Reading		
SAT Math		
SAT Writing		
SAT Essay		
ACT Composite		
ACT Math		
ACT English		
ACT Writing		

Percent of first-time, first-year (freshman) students with scores in each range:

	SAT Critical Reading	SAT Math	SAT Writing
700-800			
600-699			
500-599			
400-499			
300-399			
200-299			
	100%	100%	100%

	ACT Composite	ACT English	ACT Math
30-36			
24-29			
18-23			
12-17			
6-11			
Below 6			
	100%	100%	100%

C10. Percent of all degree-seeking, first-time, first-year (freshman) students who had high school class rank within each of the following ranges (report information for those students from whom you collected high school rank information).

Percent in top tenth of high school graduating class _____

Percent in top quarter of high school graduating class _____

Percent in top half of high school graduating class _____

Percent in bottom half of high school graduating class _____
Percent in bottom quarter of high school graduating class _____

C11. Percentage of all enrolled, degree-seeking, first-time, first-year (freshman) students who had high school grade-point averages within each of the following ranges (using 4.0 scale). Report information only for those students from whom you collected high school GPA.

Percent who had GPA of 3.75 and higher _____
Percent who had GPA between 3.50 and 3.74 _____
Percent who had GPA between 3.25 and 3.49 _____
Percent who had GPA between 3.00 and 3.24 _____

Percent who had GPA between 2.50 and 2.99 _____
Percent who had GPA between 2.0 and 2.49 _____
Percent who had GPA between 1.0 and 1.99 _____
Percent who had GPA below 1.0 _____

C12. Average high school GPA of all degree-seeking, first-time, first-year (freshman) students who submitted GPA: _____

B. Compare your stats to Naviance and the Common Data Set stats to determine if a college is a "Worst Chance," "Chance" or "Best Chance" for you.

Depending on how you compare with other students via Naviance and/or The Common Data Set, you will be able to get an idea about whether a college is a "Worst Chance," "Chance" or "Best Chance" school for you.

1. The college is a "Worst Chance" if your stats place you in the bottom 25% of all applicants.

If your scores place you in the bottom 25% of stats, your chances are worst at the college.

2. The college is a "Chance" if your stats place you at the 50% percentile of applicants.

If your scores place you in the middle 50% of stats, you have a chance, but no guarantee at the college.

3. The college is a "Best Chance" if your stats place you in the top 25% of all applicants.

If your scores place you in the top 25% of stats, your chances are best at the college. However, even perfect scores are not a guarantee at any college, especially the most selective ones.

C. Figure out what you need to get admitted to each college.

Best Chance colleges require fewer other traits/accomplishments for admission, Chance colleges require extra traits/ accomplishments, and Worst Chance colleges require significant extra accomplishments or a hook to get admitted. However, there are exceptions to every rule. Every year, unexpected students get admitted (and unfortunately rejected) without explanation.

1. "Worst Chance" schools expect you to have an extraordinary accomplishment/hook.

At the colleges where your stats fall below most admitted students, you will likely need something extraordinary to get admitted. If you have a 3.0/28 ACT and you really want to go to a specific college, but no one with less than a 3.5/32 has ever gotten admitted from your high school, you probably will not get accepted without a hook.

2. "Chance Schools" expect you to have extra traits/accomplishments.

For the colleges where your stats match the average stats, you've got a chance to get accepted, but there is also a similar possibility that you might get waitlisted or even outright rejected. The more underlined "extra" traits/accomplishments that you have, the better your chances of getting admitted.

To boost your chances:

a. Apply to different colleges from your classmates.

Apply to colleges where few people from your high school typically go. If you live in the northeast, think about heading west. Your home state might be something that can tip the scale in your favor.

b. Apply to less popular majors.

Sometimes it is easier to get accepted to less popular majors, or even as "undecided." At other colleges (like some UCs), however, some undecided majors (like undecided Engineering) have the lowest acceptance rates. Research before choosing this route.

c. Tailor your applications.

If you have a talent for juggling, and a certain college has a circus club, your unusual skill could help tip the scale towards acceptance. The more you research a college, the more you can tailor your application for that specific school. What you include on one application might be irrelevant on another – so take the time know what specific admissions officers might be looking for.

3. "Best Chance Schools" expect you to have accomplishments that raise their averages.

You have the best of acceptance at the colleges where your stats are above most admitted students (your scores appear in green on Naviance). If you have extraordinary or extra attributes, your odds will increase accordingly; you might even earn a generous merit scholarship! Demonstrate interest so that the college does not think that you are using the school as a "safety" application.

Note that even if your Naviance stats are above average for applicants from your high school, they might not be above average for the college overall, as reported by the Common Data Set. If so, the school might only be a Chance for you instead of a Best Chance.

Also note that the most selective schools are not Best Chance colleges for anyone, even those whose stats are at the top of the range. There are simply not enough seats to admit all of the seemingly perfect students who apply. If you have your sights set on an Ivy League or other most selective college, you will most likely still need a bold or highlighted trait/accomplishment, or many underlined ones, on your list from Step 1.

D. Make a spreadsheet of colleges that interest you.

Now that you have a good idea of what you are looking for in a college, and your chances at these colleges, it is time to make a spreadsheet of colleges to which you might apply. If you love it, really like it, or otherwise would be happy to attend, put it on the list.

1. List the names of colleges down the Column A.

Don't worry about ranking them yet.

2. List your chances down Column B.

Your chances are the one of the most important thing to consider. Sort the spreadsheet by this column alphabetically, expanding the election, so that "Best Chances" are at the top of the sheet and "Worst Chances" are at the bottom.

3. In the other columns, enter other characteristics that are important to you from Step 5.

Include thins like Majors, Selectivity, Size, Location, Type, Cost, Housing, Transportation, Minimum Requirements, Curriculum, Retention Rates, Reputation, Greek Life, Graduation Rates, Job Placement Rates, Extracurriculars and AP/IB Credits.

STEP 6 CHECKLIST

DETERMINE YOUR CHANCES AT THE SCHOOLS THAT INTEREST YOU

o Use your high school's Naviance webpage and The Common Data Set to compare yourself to other applicants

o Compare your stats to Naviance and the Common Data Set stats to determine if a college is a "Worst Chance," "Chance" or "Best Chance" for you.

o Figure out what you need to get admitted to each college

o Make a spreadsheet of colleges that interest you

VII

Yield Matters

STEP 7 - DEMONSTRATE YOUR INTEREST

(Target Date: February of Junior Year through Acceptance)

Colleges are very interested in raising their yield - the percentage of students who enroll at the college after they are offered acceptance. The higher a college's yield, the better the school's rank and reputation. It is therefore important for admissions officers to believe that if they accept you, you will attend, since colleges often "protect yield" by rejecting qualified students who they do believe will not enroll.

A good way to tip the scale in your favor is to demonstrate your genuine interest in the school to admissions officers, and prove that you are not using their college as a "safety" application. Often, a decision between two otherwise equal candidates will be made based on which student is more likely to enroll. The student who has demonstrated more interest will likely be the one who ends up in the "yes" pile.

Colleges that report to the Common Data Set disclose how much emphasis they place on students' demonstrated interest. If a college does not publish this information, or even if they claim that they do not track interest, assume that most schools, except the most selective schools, actually do track your interest. These colleges keep a file and note the different ways that you have demonstrated your interest.

A. Take formal tours at all of the schools on your list that are within four hours driving distance.

Colleges within a four-hour drive from your home expect you to visit their campus to prove that you are interested in their school. If you your visits are limited, focus on your "Chance" schools first, since demonstrating your interest at these colleges will likely have the biggest impact on your admission. Keep in mind that the further you travel, the more interest you demonstrate. An informative site about college day trips is:

http://www.daytripperuniversity.com

1. Take formal tours.

Rather than touring on your own, sign up for formal tours so that school can track your visit. If not possible, sign in at the admissions office before your self-tour.

2. Visit while classes are in session.

To get a good feel of the vibe on campus, do not visit during college breaks, or exam periods when student might be uncharacteristically stressed. As you walk around, ask yourself: Is the campus overly crowded or empty? How are students dressed? Would you fit in?

3. Ask questions during the tour.

Take time to get answers to any questions that you might have. A good question to ask, if you can't think of anything specific, is "what is unique about the school that is not mentioned on the website?" The answer that you receive could provide you material for any supplemental essays. Here are some others:

http://www.usnews.com/education/blogs/thecollegesolution/2010/10/19/36-questions-to-ask-on-a-college-visit/

—How much time do students typically spend on homework?
—How much writing and reading are expected?
—What is the average class size of introductory classes?
—How widely used are teaching assistants on your campus?
—What is the average class size of upper-division courses?

Academic Perks

—What opportunities are there for undergraduate research?
—How many students participate in undergraduate research?
—Is there a culminating senior year experience?
—Do you have an honors college?
—Do you have a learning community or other freshman experience?

Financial Aid

—What is your average financial aid package?
—What is the typical breakdown of loans versus grants?
—What percentage of financial need does the school typically meet?
—What is the average merit award?
—What percentages of students receive college grants?

—What is the average college debt that students leave with?
—What work-study opportunities are there?

Graduation Track Record

—What is your four-year graduation rate?
—What is your five-year graduation rate?
—What does it take to graduate in four years?
—What percentage of freshmen return for sophomore year?

Academic Support

—What type of tutoring program do you have?
—How do you provide academic advice to students?
—Do you have a writing center and how do I access it?
—What kind of learning disability resources do you have?

Outside Opportunities

—How many students at the college get internships?
—What percentages of students study abroad?
—What type of career services do you have?

Student Life

—What kinds of dorm choices are there?
—What percentage of student live on campus?
—How long are dorm accommodations guaranteed?
—How many students live on campus?
—Do most students go home on the weekend?
—What percentage of the study body belongs to a sorority or fraternity?
—What activities are offered to students?
—What clubs do you have on campus?

4. Sit in on a class.

If you have a particular interest in a class, email the professor and ask to sit in during your visit. Arrive early, introduce yourself, and spend a few minutes discussing your interest in the college. This could provide material for supplemental essays.

5. Eat in the dining hall.

Most colleges allow non-students to purchase meals in their dining halls.

Make note of the food offerings and general atmosphere. Are there healthy options? Are lots of students eating by themselves? Is it clean?

6. Visit the Student Union.

The student Union is usually a popular centralized location. Look for comfy seating areas that foster socialization. Are students sitting together and chatting? Are they smiling? Could you picture yourself here?

7. Visit the rec center/gym.

If you are allowed to enter the student rec center/gym, check it out. Are many students using the facilities? Is it updated? Would you feel comfortable using it?

8. Read a copy of the Campus Newspaper.

Read through the campus newspaper to see what's going on at the college. What is the tone of the publication? Does it make the school sound like a place that you could call "home?"

9. Visit the surrounding area.

Tours do not usually include the surrounding area. Take a drive around the outskirts of the campus and check out off-campus housing locations. Is it a convenient, nice and safe place to shop, eat and live?

10. Do not write off a school unless you are sure that it is not a good fit.

If you are unsure about how you feel because the weather is bad, or your tour guide is annoying, or you are just in a cranky mood, do not write off a college that otherwise meets your criteria. A second visit later in the process might give you a completely different view on things. If, though, you are sure that you would not be happy at the school, take it off you list.

11. Send thank-you notes.

If anyone took time to meet with you or answer your questions, send them a quick "thank you." Spellcheck! The note will likely be kept in your admissions file.

B. Sign up for info sessions at your high school.

Colleges often send local admission reps to high schools to hold informational sessions. These are sometimes the very people who will be reading your essays. It is a great opportunity to make a good first impression on admissions.

Arrive early if possible, introduce yourself, and tell the rep that you are very interested in the college. Ask a specific question about the school that can not be easily answered via their website. Afterwards, email a "thank you" and say that you are excited to apply to the college.

C. Request info.

College websites can be a wealth of information. Opt-in for emails, snail mail, college blogs, webinars, and anything else available. If they offer it, sign up for it.

D. Request an interview.

Some colleges require interviews for specific majors. Others offer interviews to anyone who asks for one. If a college offers on or off-site interviews, request one.

Dress conservatively and have questions prepared to ask about the school. Bring your resume and transcript. Arrive early, but not more than 15 minutes early.

E. Take virtual tours.

If you have not taken an actual tour, view the online tour. Even if you have taken an actual tour, still view the official online virtual tour. Some colleges track this online activity.

F. Open and forward emails that you receive from colleges.

Colleges can tell if you delete an email without ever reading it. If you want a college to note your interest, do not only open any emails that you receive from them, but also forward them to someone else, like your parents. Apparently, some colleges track these things, too.

G. Contact your admissions rep with valid questions.

Ask your guidance counselor for the contact information for specific colleges' admissions reps, if you don't already have the information. Contact the reps to indicate your interest in their school, and to ask any valid questions that you have that can not be easily answered via the college website. Do not, however, annoy these reps with repeated requests for information.

STEP 7 CHECKLIST

DEMONSTRATE YOUR INTEREST

- Take formal tours at all of the schools on your list that are within four hours driving distance

- Sign up for info sessions at your high school

- Request information

- Request an interview

- Take virtual tours

- Open and forward emails that you receive from colleges

- Contact your admissions rep with valid questions

VIII

Image Matters

STEP 8 – CLEAN UP YOUR SOCIAL MEDIA ACCOUNTS

(Target Date: March of Junior Year)

Colleges will choose the student with a better "image," when given a choice between otherwise identical applicants. Sometimes it comes down to posted pictures of a charitable event vs. posted pictures of beer bottles. Do not become one of the many students every year that is denied admittance or rescinded after acceptance due to inappropriate photos, language or attitude on social media.

The Internet is forever and unforgiving. Once you post, tweet or snap something, no matter what your privacy settings, expect that anyone, including admissions officers, can see it. Competitive "friends" with screenshots of other students' inappropriate photos or statements have been known to forward them to colleges. Admissions officers also perform Internet searches when choosing whom to admit and reject.

A. Do an Internet search on yourself.

Place your legal name in the search bar and see what comes up. Next search any your nicknames/screen names. Are you proud of what pops up? If not, take steps to change the results.

http://thefreethoughtproject.com/google-yourself-deep-search-instead-brace-results/

B. Delete all old social media accounts, photos and posts that do not portray you positively.

Delete any Facebook, Instagram, Twitter, and other social media accounts that do not portray you in a positive way. If you insist on keeping your social media accounts: update the privacy settings to private; use an alias and not your full legal name; and in the very least, delete pictures or posts involving anything illegal or objectionable, such as profanity, weapons, nudity, and anything else that could cost you an acceptance.

C. Un-tag yourself from other peoples' social media accounts.

It won't matter that your own accounts are squeaky clean if you have made controversial comments or posted inappropriate pictures elsewhere on the Internet. Refrain from posting or posing in ways that could come back to haunt you. Also, ask your parents not to post any revealing information about you on their accounts that might scare off admissions officers; you might be surprised at what they are posting about you.

D. Create new social media accounts.

Create new social media accounts that you can link to your college applications, and post on them regularly. Some colleges acknowledge using social media not only to reject applicants, but also to find students to accept. If your fill your "official" Facebook page with positive messages and pictures of you volunteering your time, it might tip the scale towards your acceptance.

Use your legal name as your screen name so that colleges can find you. Refrain from posting about your "number one college," your acceptances, or anything else that might damage your image to specific admissions officers on these pages. Remember that every college wants to believe that it is your first choice!

E. Create a college-only email address.

Create a professional email that you will only use to communicate with colleges. For example, you can use your "firstlastname@Gmail.com" if it is available. Do not to use something juvenile or improper, such as "cutiepie123@"," "fastdriver@" or "ILOVE WEED@." Check this account frequently to make sure that you promptly reply to any college correspondence.

F. Create logins at college websites.

Create online accounts at colleges that allow you to. Use a professional user name, such as your "firstlastname." Keep track of your login information, and login periodically.

G. Be active on college social media accounts.

"Like" college social media accounts and posts. Follow, "re-tweet" them and comment on them, but sound intelligent when you do so. Also, realize that if you can see their account, they can probably see yours, too.

H. Create a resume.

Some colleges ask you to attach a resume to their application. Others will review a resume if you attach one. Keep it to one page, and concisely list any valuable experience on it.

I. Create a LinkedIn profile.

LinkedIn is an amazing way to promote yourself. Once you create an account, try to make connections with teachers, bosses, and other people who might be willing to endorse you on the site. Upload your resume and anything else that makes you stand out, and link your profile on your application if possible. See:

https://university.linkedin.com/linkedin-for-students

http://www.abc2news.com/news/education/more-schools-are-checking-linkedin-for-college-applications

J. Create your own webpage that showcases your accomplishments.

You can help make your accomplishments stand out further by publicizing them on your own website. If you have arranged for an interview with a local TV station about your passion or submitted a news article about your talent with your photo attached, showcase it here and link the site to your social media accounts and college applications. There are many free website/hosting options available.

K. Do not share your logins/passwords with anyone.

Never share your password with anyone, even your "best friend." Former BFFs have been known to login to Facebook under their friend's account and post nasty comments that colleges could misinterpret. And, imagine the damage that could be done by a former friend who logs into your Common App account and changes your essay.

L. Secure your electronics.

Make sure that your phone, laptop and other electronics are all password protected for the same reasons as above. Also, log out of accounts before loaning out your electronics. If you are logged into a site, and someone "borrows" your electronics, s/he could access your important accounts.

STEP 8 CHECKLIST

CLEAN UP YOUR SOCIAL MEDIA ACCOUNTS

- o Do an Internet search on yourself

- o Delete all accounts, photos and posts that do not portray you positively

- o Un-tag yourself from other peoples' social media accounts

- o Create new social media profiles

- o Create a college-only email address

- o Create logins at college websites

- o Be active on college social media accounts

- o Create a resume

- o Create a LinkedIn profile

- o Create your own webpage that showcases your accomplishments

- o Do not share your logins/passwords with anyone

- o Secure your electronics

IX

The Ratio of Applications Matters

STEP 9 – PLAN TO APPLY TO THE RIGHT AMOUNT OF COLLEGES

(Target Date: April of Junior Year)

Many students submit an excessive amount of applications because they mistakenly believe that the greater number of applications, the better their chances to get accepted to more schools. However, if they only apply to "Worst Chance" schools, they may not get accepted to any.

No matter how many applications you can only attend one at a time. So, your goal should be to get accepted into three affordable colleges that you would be happy to attend, at least one of which is close to home. To achieve your goal, focus on the ratio, not number, of your applications.

A. Plan to apply to at least three affordable Best Chance colleges that you would be happy to attend.

Most students, except for those applying Early Decision, hope to have at least a few options to choose from come decision time. If you can only afford or fit in three applications, they should all be for affordable Best Chance colleges that you would be happy to attend if admitted.

B. Plan to apply to at least one affordable Best Chance, close-to-home college that you would be happy to attend.

You can never predict what might happen during senior year of high school. Sometimes, applicants who had wished to go far away have a change of heart. Other times, students need to remain close for a different reason. Make sure that alt least one of your affordable Best Chance applications is close-to-home.

C. Plan to apply to two affordable "Chance" colleges for every one "Worst Chance" application.

Your odds of admission, if you do not have a hook, are low at you your Worst Chance colleges. Do not let anyone convince you otherwise. Your odds of admission if you do not have a hook or significant "extra" accomplishments or traits, are about 50/50 at your Chance colleges. To keep your options open, plan

71

to apply to two Chance colleges for every one Worst Chance application.

D. Do not plan to apply to more than 12 colleges.

The Common App has made it easy for students to apply to a high number colleges. However, more colleges are now requiring supplemental materials, requiring extra time and effort. It is a better idea to perfect a smaller number of submissions than to submit a greater amount of mediocre applications. Try very hard to limit yourself to 12 applications.

Examples that follow the above-described ratio:

Worst Chance	Chance	Best Chance colleges
3	6	3
2	4	3
1	2	3
0	0	3

E. Plan to apply to only as many colleges that you can afford to submit.

College applications are expensive. Don't forget to factor in the additional costs associated to send score reports and also CSS financial forms to the colleges that require them. All totaled, the most selective college applications add up to over $100 each.

Many colleges waive fees for students who cannot afford them:

https://bigfuture.collegeboard.org/get-in/applying-101/college-application-fee-waivers/participating-colleges

F. Plan to apply to only as many colleges that you have time to submit.

The more time you have to spend on each application, the better. Some require essays and short answers; others do not. Some essays can be used for multiple applications, while others will be too specific to do so.

You will not know how much time and effort an application will take until you do it. Just know that many can take several days, and plan accordingly. Never rush an application!

G. Be optimistic, but realistic.

It is okay to dream big as long as you understand the realities of college admissions. First, it is oftentimes random. Many applicants have been rejected from their Chance colleges simply because there are too many qualified candidates, leaving admissions officers to seemingly pick students out of a hat.

Other times, students are rejected from their Best Chance colleges because admissions officers believe that the student has no intention to attend. Yield protection is real, especially at private colleges. If you have not demonstrated any interest, even above-average GPA and scores might not get you admitted.

Next, there are not as many open slots as you imagine. For example, a certain Ivy League college might accept an entering freshman class of 1,500 students. However, almost 1,000 of those openings will be offered to hooked athletes, legacies and underrepresented minorities during early action, and 75% of those offered acceptance will enroll. So, before admissions even reviews your regular decision application, 1/2 of the class will already be filled. You now have 750 chances.

50% of those slots will be filled by the opposite sex. You're down to 375, until you learn that for diversity's sake, 75% of the remaining openings are slated for different races, regions and religions. You and the 29,000 other remaining applicants are now competing for less than 100 chances to get accepted.

When broken down, you can see how difficult it is to get admitted at the most selective colleges. While you can still dream, you need to be realistic. You might win the lottery, but have a backup plan if you don't.

H. Decide which colleges are your final choices, and update your spreadsheet.

Review everything that you have learned up until this point, and pick which schools make up your final choices. Once you have determined which applications to submit, update your spreadsheet. Add extra columns for other important things like scholarship due dates, scores required to be sent, and additional required essays.

STEP 9 CHECKLIST

PLAN TO APPLY TO THE RIGHT AMOUNT OF COLLEGES

o Plan to apply to at least three affordable Best Chance colleges that you would be happy to attend

o Plan to apply to at least one affordable Best Chance, close-to-home college that you would be happy to attend

o Plan to apply to two affordable "Chance" colleges for every one "Worst Chance" application

o Do not plan to apply to more than 12 colleges

o Plan to apply to only as many colleges that you can afford to submit

o Plan to apply to only as many colleges that you have time to submit

o Be optimistic, but realistic

o Decide which colleges are your final choices and update your spreadsheet

X

<u>Timing Matters</u>

STEP 10 – DECIDE IF YOU WILL APPLY EARLY DECISION, EARLY ACTION, OR EARLY

(Target Date: May of Junior Year)

Colleges often reward the early bird with the worm. The earliest applicants usually have the best chances of acceptance, merit and financial aid. Plan to have all of your applications completed by October 1ˢᵗ of your senior year.

The Common Application opens on August 1ˢᵗ. Before that date, you can create your Common App account, and add your selected schools to it. You can also decide on which colleges you will apply Early Decision, Early Action, and Regular Decision.

A. Apply "Early Decision" (ED) if you are 100% sure that you want to attend the college, can afford it if admitted, and do not require a boost from senior year.

Some colleges allow students to apply Early Decision, which is binding. This means that if you select the ED option and complete your entire application by a specific early date (usually by 11/1, but sometimes even earlier), the college will decide on your application by a specific early date (oftentimes in December). If the college accepts you, you agree to withdraw all other open applications and enroll at the ED college.

   1. **You can only apply to one ED college.**

   The ED contract is binding, so you can only apply ED to one college. Only use this option if you are 100% certain that you want to attend if admitted.

   2. Applying ED might hurt your financial aid/merit package.

   ED colleges might not be as generous with aid because they know that you are obligated to attend if admitted, and therefore do not need to lure you in with offers of more money. Only apply ED if you are sure that it will be affordable.

   3. Applying ED might boost your admissions chances.

Applying ED is the greatest form of demonstrating interest. And, ED admission rates are higher than regular decision rates. However, these numbers include recruited athletes and other hooked students, so the percentages are not as great as they seem.

4. Most high schools require that you sign an acknowledgement of the ED contract, since breaking ED can negatively impact a high school's relationship with a college.

If you break the ED contract, your high school will likely refuse to send out transcripts/letters of recommendation/etc. to any other colleges for you.

5. You can get out of the ED contract if the financial package offered by the college does not meet your needs, but you might still face consequences.

If you cannot afford to attend the college, you can get out of the contract. However, there is still a risk that your high school might not assist you with other applications or that other colleges might be hesitant to accept you. It is best to only apply ED to an affordable school.

6. Applying ED might limit your ability to simultaneously apply to other schools via Early Action.

ED colleges may prohibit any simultaneous Early Action applications (other than at permitted state universities, or for certain scholarship requirements). If you don't want to wait for acceptances until April, and have several other EA options, it might be best not to limit yourself to one early decision application.

7. ED colleges will not factor in your senior grades/scores.

Your senior year grades/scores will likely not be available for ED review. If your application could use a boost from senior year, you are probably better off not applying ED. A great first semester senior year could tip the scale towards your acceptance.

8. If your application is incomplete, it will be moved to regular decision.

Although some colleges do allow for a grace period of approximately a week to receive supplemental materials such as transcripts, test scores and letters of recommendation, they all expect that your portion of the application be submitted by the deadline. Otherwise, it will be moved to regular decision.

9. You can change your mind about applying ED before the college makes a decision by contacting admissions and asking to be moved to regular decision.

Colleges will move your application to regular decision if requested. The move might have an impact on your chances, as your demonstrated interest drops.

10. Some colleges offer a second round of Early Decision called "ED II."

ED II is a later round of ED applications after the first round of Early Decisions, but before regular decisions. It is also binding. Only apply ED II if it is affordable and you are 100% sure about attending if admitted.

11. If you are not accepted ED, you will be rejected or deferred.

Some colleges outright reject most ED applicants who are not accepted early. Others "defer" most of the non-accepted ED applicants to the regular decision pool. Applicants speculate as to whether deferred students have a better chance of acceptance in the regular pool than regular applicants, but it is almost impossible to know if they do. The CDS reports ED and EA plans in question C21.

B. Apply "Early Action" (EA) to every school that allows it, if you do not need a boost from senior year grades/scores.

Some colleges allow students to apply Early Action, which is not binding. This means that if you select the early action option and apply by a specific early date (usually 11/1 but sometimes even earlier), the college will decide on your application by a specific early date. If you are accepted, you will have until May 1ˢᵗ to decide.

1. Applying EA might boost your admissions chances.

Applying EA demonstrates interest. And, EA admit rates are higher than regular decision rates. However, these numbers also include recruited athletes and other hooked students, so the percentages are not as great as they seem.

2. Applying EA will not hurt your chances of scoring financial/merit aid.

Since EA is not binding, colleges do not have you "locked in." There is no fear that colleges will offer you less aid because they might still feel the need to lure you in with money.

3. Applying EA might limit your ability to simultaneously apply EA to other colleges.

Some EA colleges only offer Single Choice Early Action (SCEA), which restricts students from applying to any other EA college (except certain state universities, or private colleges that require EA application for scholarship consideration). If you apply to a SCEA college, you will limit your ability to apply EA to most other colleges.

4. Colleges will not factor in your senior grades/scores if you apply EA.

Your senior year grades/scores will likely not be available for EA review. If your application could use a boost from senior year, you are probably better off applying regular decision. A great first semester senior year could tip the scale towards your acceptance.

C. Apply by October 1ˢᵗ to "Regular Decision" colleges.

If you choose not to apply ED or EA, still apply early, especially since many scholarship deadlines are prior to application deadlines. Submit all applications no later than October1ˢᵗ. Colleges will not be obliged to render a decision by a certain date, but some will let you know sooner than others.

1. Colleges with "Rolling Admissions" (RA) make decisions on a rolling basis.

Some RA colleges decide on applications in the order in which they are received, while others pick and choose by major or other criteria. You might receive a decision in a few days, or may not hear back for months. You will have until May 1ˢᵗ to decide, if accepted.

2. Colleges without Rolling Admissions will announce all decisions on a certain future date, usually by April 1ˢᵗ.

Applying earlier than the deadline for these colleges probably will not give you an advantage. However, it will prove to admissions that you are organized and driven, which might impress them.

STEP 10 CHECKLIST

DECIDE IF YOU WILL APPLY EARLY DECISION, EARLY ACTION OR EARLY

o Apply "Early Decision" (ED) if you are 100% sure that you want to attend the college, can afford it if admitted, and do not require a boost from senior year

o Apply "Early Action" (EA) to every school that allows it, if you do not need a boost from senior year grades/scores

o Apply by October 1ˢᵗ to "Regular Decision" colleges

Essays and Short Answers Matter

STEP 11 – WRITE UNIQUE AND MEMORABLE SHORT ANSWERS AND ESSAYS

(Target Date: Summer Before Senior Year)

Admissions officers fight for students who they "know" and like. Your essays and short answers should therefore be so unique to you that they make the reader feels like s/he knows and likes you. Use your writing to reveal your story and personality, and tell colleges know why you would make a great addition to their class.

Some schools do not require any essays or short answers, but most do expect at least one personal statement. Others request multiple essays and short answers. Know exactly what is expected.

A. Start thinking about essays early.

New Common App essay prompts are usually released in January or February every year. You do not need to wait until then to start thinking about what you want to write. More important than any specific prompt is what you want your story to be. When an essay idea pops into your head, jot it down. You can fit your story into a prompt later.

B. Read what worked, and did not work, for others.

Here are some examples:

https://apply.jhu.edu/apply/essays-that-worked

https://www.conncoll.edu/admission/apply/essays-that-worked/

http://admissions.tufts.edu/apply/advice/past-essays/common-application-essays/

http://www.businessinsider.com/high-school-senior-who-got-into-5-ivy-league-schools-shares-her-admissions-essay-2016-4

http://www.road2college.com/use-the-secrets-of-screenwriting-to-write-your-college-essay/

http://www.road2college.com/43-phrases-you-should-never-use-in-a-college-admission-essay/

C. Be unique.

Your essays and short answers should be so unique to you, that if you dropped them on the floor of your high school, a classmate who picked them up and read them would immediately know that they belonged to you.

D. Be Memorable.

Make your essay memorable enough for Admissions officers to give you a nickname.

Admissions officers often assign nicknames to applicants as they debate on whom to admit. The girl who wrote her essay about her love for climbing trees despite her fear of heights might become the "fearless climber." A boy who wrote about being mocked by his friends for escorting his elderly neighbors across a busy street every morning before school might be referred to as "the cross-walker."

Since "varsity athlete" could apply to hundreds or more applicants, generic sports stories do not usually make great essay topics. However, a five-foot tall basketball player who overcame the hardship on the court might be a memorable "little guard."

If you already have a nickname that describes you well, this could be a good place to start. For example, a student who is known as "The Human Calculator" might write about his unique talent of solving complicated math problems in his head and how it helped to earn him not only a nickname but also several prominent awards. "The Gazelle" could explain how her years of dance training helped her overcome an accident-related injury and fostered her passion to teach ballet to young children

E. Be like-able.

Write about things that will make admissions officers want to accept you. Don't choose a topic that portrays you in a negative way. Colleges will not be impressed if you tell them that you have always been a bully, but recently changed your ways.

Also, steer clear from controversial or uncomfortable topics. Things like politics,

81

religion, and bodily functions have gotten otherwise excellent applicants into trouble. Remember that if the person reading your essay does not agree with your particular views, or find farting to be as funny as you do, your essay might land your application in the rejected pile.

F. Be real.

Most admissions officers can see right through disingenuous essays, including ones that were not written by an actual high school student. Do not ask someone else to write your essays for you or plagiarize someone else's work. There is software out there that will catch you if you do.

Do not brag about building houses during a one-time short trip to a disadvantaged country unless you also have a list of local charity work. Admissions officers are not impressed with vacation volunteering.

Also, don't make up your story. Admissions officers have been known to verify essay facts. If the truth is revealed during an interview with you or a call to your guidance counselor, you could be rejected, or rescinded after acceptance.

Most times, the best essays are about simple yet unique and memorable things about you and your everyday life. Be yourself and use words that you normally use – not a thesaurus or clichés. Let your personality shine through!

G. Write about you.

Admissions officers want to learn more about you, not about your grandmother or your best friend who inspires you. Although it is fine to mention others, the focus of the essay must be on you. Tell them your story, and make them like and want you.

H. Follow the word count (and any other instructions).

If the instructions limit you to 650 words, or 150 characters, follow the directions. Some applications might not submit your response unless it fits. Even if it is submitted, you will have proven to admissions that you either cannot follow, or choose to disregard, directions.

I. Grab the reader's attention right away.

The job of reading essays can get very mundane, very quickly. Your essay will stand out to admissions officers if the first sentence or paragraph grabs their attention. The best essays are the ones that readers don't want to put down:

J. Use a common theme throughout the essays and short answers.

Creating a common theme of who you are throughout your entire application will reinforce your story. Instead of approaching each essay/question independently, use every blank to reinforce the common image that your wish to portray. If you hope to be remembered as the "winning quiz bowl contestant who always put everyone above herself," every writing section should remind readers of that person.

K. Include specific college references.

Refer to the specific college in your essays and short answers. If you are using a main essay for more than one application, you can tailor it to different schools. The Common App allows you to edit your essay after you submit each application.

L. Include, if possible, adversity and obstacles that you have overcome.

Colleges give "extra points" to applicants who have faced adversity and overcome obstacles. Some examples include students who have succeeded after battling a disability or illness, being homeless, coming from a broken home, being bullied, or suffering from racial, cultural, sexual orientation, or other discrimination. If you have risen above something that otherwise could have brought you down, weave the experience into your essay to help make you a more desirable candidate.

Note that some hardships might be best left unmentioned. Topics such as living with mental illness and tackling drug addiction are things that could scare off some admissions officers. Do not paint yourself as a potential liability for a college.

M. Pay special attention to supplemental essays.

Many colleges require additional essays, including "Why (our school)?" Use the space to be specific about why they should want to admit you, and not to spit back to them information about the college.

Do not write: it is a great school; it is in a good location; my mom is making me apply. Instead, use information that you have learned about the school from friends, relatives, informational sessions and tours to explain how you would succeed at the college. They already know everything about them; this is about you.

For example, if the college offers a unique major that you love, and you sat in on a class with a certain professor whom you admire, write about that. If you have always dreamed, since attending football games on campus with your alumni parents as a child, of playing tuba for their marching band, or becoming the team mascot, tell them. If your favorite author/scientist/actor is a graduate of your intended program and you already own multiple "this school" t-shirts because you can't imagine attending any other university, let them know.

N. Do not underestimate the importance of short answers.

Many students believe that because short answers are short, they do not require a lot of thought or time. This could not be further from the truth. Even if full sentences are not required, never rush through this section.

Keep your common theme in mind. Also be mindful of what the school is looking for. Be honest, but try to tailor your responses for the college.

For example, if you are applying to a very liberal campus, you might not choose to describe yourself on this application in three words as "republican, conservative, red." Better responses for this particular school might be "proud, political, activist." Also remember that admissions officers read thousands of these answers, so anytime you can come up with something original, it will help you stand out.

O. Do not share your essays with your classmates, or post them publicly.

Keep your essay topics to yourself. Unfortunately, other students, including your friends, are your competition. You never know who might choose to steal your idea or essay.

Similarly, never post your essay on a blog, board, or anywhere else. Colleges regularly use software to determine if essays have been plagiarized. Even if no one has taken your essay, your own words posted online could raise issues for you.

P. Use "special circumstance" essays to your advantage.

If there is a place to describe "special circumstances," use it to explain anything that may otherwise give admissions officers pause about your application. If you have made any mistakes, own up to them and describe how you have learned from them; do not place blame on anyone for your circumstances. If there is no specific section for special circumstances, use the "additional information" section, if there is one, for topics including:

1. Dips in grades

If your GPA suffered at some point, or if you received a particularly bad grade in one class, it will benefit you to explain what happened. For example, if you had mono, describe how the illness made it difficult for you to keep up with your work, but also forced you to become a more organized student in the end. If you received a "D" in Calculus, don't complain that your teacher was terrible (even if s/he was) but instead, talk about what you learned from the disappointment and how you improved as a result.

2. Hardship

If you experienced any hardship during high school that you have not addressed elsewhere in the application, speak to it here. For example, if you had to take three separate buses for two hours to get to and from school, explain how that made it difficult for you get enough sleep and focus on your homework. Likewise, if you were required to work 20 hours every week to help contribute to your family, discuss it.

3. Absences/Tardiness

If you were chronically late or absent, and it is documented on your transcript, colleges will want to know why. Saying that you were tired or just didn't feel like going will be helpful. However, if you have an excuse such as an illness that required frequent daytime doctor visits, or the responsibility of getting your six siblings ready for school every day, make note of it.

4. Change of school

If you moved during high school and it affected you in some way, explain how. If you did not move, but changed schools within your district for some other reason, it also may not be a bad idea to let admissions know that it was not because you were expelled from your prior school (if it was not).

5. Disciplinary issues

Although some applications do not ask, the Common App and many other applications inquire, amongst other things, if the student has ever been found responsible for a disciplinary violation during high school that resulted in a disciplinary action such as "probation, suspension, removal, dismissal or expulsion."

The student's guidance counselor will usually be asked the same question, and also for an explanation. Some high school policies prohibit the counselor from answering. A student must then decide if s/he will be truthful in answering the question.

Since a cover up is usually worse than the crime itself, tell the truth. Even if the discipline is not documented on your transcript, or will not be disclosed by the school, a disgruntled classmate could alert colleges about the infraction.

On the other hand, if a college does not ask the question, or if the discipline is not specifically named, there is no requirement to divulge the information.

For disciplinary actions that must be included in the application, it is best to be upfront about what happened, take responsibility for it, and describe what was learned from it. Something that occurred during freshman year will be easier to explain away than a more recent incident. However, colleges understand that students make mistakes and often overlook disciplinary issues that appear to be a single deviation.

It will important to admissions that your description of the event matches your counselor's description. Ask your counselor to read your explanation, determine if s/he agrees with it, and if not, request help to edit it as necessary.

No matter what happens with the counselor, it is impossible to know how colleges will react. It is therefore imperative that you apply to at least three Best Chance colleges that do not ask about disciplinary matters. Many public universities, and some private colleges who do not use the Common App, do not inquire.

Q. Do not leave anything blank.

There is no such thing as an "optional" essay or answer on a college application. If a college gives you an option, take it. If you don't, you will appear less interested than the others who do.

If there is an "additional info" section that requests other relevant information, use it. Although you should not simply repeat what you have already stated elsewhere, it can be used to further explain things already included on the application. For example, if you won an award, use this space to explain its significance or what steps led up to the win.

You can also use this space to link to any pertinent webpages. For instance, if you have written a news article that was published in your local paper, provide the link. Or, if you have a LinkedIn profile, link it to this space.

R. Edit, edit some more, and then edit again.

Your best essay cannot be written in one day. First, create a draft. Edit it repeatedly until it is amazing. Next, put it down for a day, come back to it, and edit some more.

Then, read it out loud. Does your story demand attention from the very beginning? Does it flow easily? Does it paint a good picture of who you are? Is it memorable? Does it support a good nickname?

Finally, ask your favorite English teacher or brilliant adult friend read it to check for errors.

When you are fully satisfied with your essay, feel free use it for multiple applications, if fitting. However, be very careful when copying and pasting if your writing contains any specific school references. USC will not want to hear that you "can't wait to wear UCLA's Bruin Blue."

STEP 11 CHECKLIST

WRITE UNIQUE AND MEMORABLE SHORT ANSWERS AND ESSAYS

o Start thinking about essays early

o Read what worked, and did not work, for others

o Be unique

o Be memorable

o Be like-able

o Be real

o Write about you

o Follow the word count (and any other instructions)

o Grab the reader's attention right away

o Use a common theme throughout the essays and short answers

o Include specific college references

o Include, if possible, obstacles that you have overcome

o Pay special attention to supplemental essays

o Do not underestimate the importance of short answers

o Do not share your essays with your classmates, or post them publicly

o Use "Special Circumstance Essays" to your advantage

o Do not leave anything blank

o Edit, edit some more, and then edit again

XII

Application Details Matter

STEP 12 – APPLY CAREFULLY

(Target Date: Summer Before Senior Year)

You are now ready to begin filling out your applications! Pay careful attention to the details of each and every application. Different colleges do things differently.

A. Use the correct application.

First, confirm that you applying to the correct college. Sometimes, different colleges with similar names cause confusion. For example, The University of Miami in Florida is not Miami University in Ohio; Cornell University in New York is not Cornell College in Iowa; Columbia College in New York City is not Columbia College of Chicago.

Also be sure that you are using the preferred application. Some colleges give you a choice of applications to use, but note that they prefer one instead of another. Always choose their preferred application, even if it will take more work or time to complete. If colleges do not seem to care which application you choose, it is usually easiest to stick with what you are acquainted with, which will likely be the Common Application.

B. Follow all of the directions.

Many applications have very specific instructions. Just because you have done something one way for an earlier application does not mean that it should be done the same for the next. Read everything on each application carefully and thoroughly.

C. Use your legal name and correct Social Security number.

Many applications get lost in the process due to mistakes in names and/or Social Security numbers. Use the name that is on your birth certificate on every document, even if you don't otherwise regularly use it. Check that your Social Security number is accurate on applications and financial forms.

D. Self-report your grades, if necessary.

Some colleges require that you self-report your high school grades as a part of their application. They might require that you enter the information into a separate portal, or in the same portal as the application itself. It can be a tedious and often times confusing process. Ask you guidance office for help, if needed.

E. Decide on a Major.

Choosing a Major on a college application can impact your admissions decision and the potential to change your mind at a later date. Before you decide, it is important to confirm how Majors are declared at each college, how easily Majors can be changed, and which Majors have the lowest/highest acceptance rates. A good strategy is to choose different Majors for different applications, as necessary.

F. Decide on whether to ask for financial aid at each college.

Many applications ask if you require financial aid. Some college are "need-blind," which means that your need will not affect their decision to admit you. Requiring aid, however, might make it harder for you to get admitted to a college that is not need-blind. If you definitely will not require need-based aid to attend a college, do not request it.

G. Submit a supplemental portfolio when required, requested or allowed.

Some colleges require a portfolio, while others request or allow one. If required, you must submit one. If not required, you will need to decide whether a portfolio might help or hurt your chances. Never submit a mediocre supplement.

STEP 12 CHECKLIST

APPLY CARELULLY

o Use the correct application

o Follow all of the directions

o Use your legal name and correct Social Security number

o Self-report your grades, if necessary

o Decide on a Major

o Decide on whether to ask for financial aid at each college

o Submit a supplemental portfolio when required, requested or allowed

APPENDICES

Appendix 1

Important Things To Do After Applying

After submitting your application:

A. Keep a copy of your submission confirmation.

Screenshot and/or print your "submission received" page. Additionally, if you did not receive an emailed confirmation, login to the college portal to confirm that your application was received. Follow up if there was a glitch. The student, not the parent, should make any necessary calls to admissions.

B. Pay for the application or request a fee waiver.

After submitting your application, you will be asked to make a payment. Sometimes, in the excitement of hitting submit, this step is not completed. Make sure that your payment is accepted.

C. Keep a copy of your receipt of payment.

Screenshot and/or print the "payment received" screen. Also look for a payment confirmation at your college email address. Any missing confirmations warrant a call to admissions by the student.

D. Review your transcript and send copies to colleges.

After making a final review of your transcript for errors, etc., ask that your guidance office send copies to colleges. Some high schools require several weeks' notice for transcript requests, so do not wait until deadlines pass.

E. Update Naviance.

Many high schools require students to update their Naviance account throughout the process. Some will not release transcripts until a status is updated to "submitted." If your school uses Naviance, keep it up to date.

F. Submit score reports.

If you have not already sent free score reports, you must pay to send official score reports for each college application. To do so, login to the SAT or ACT website, and choose which scores to send. Double-check the college code to ensure that you send to the intended school.

If a college allows for "score choice," you can pick and choose which scores to report. For example, you can decide to send one or more ACT or SAT scores, or any combination of the two, keeping "super-scoring" in mind. If, on the other hand, the college requires all scores from either the ACT or SAT, you must send all that exist. Finally, if the college requires all scores from all tests, which is rare, you must send every SAT and ACT score that exists in your records.

Here is a list of SAT score use practices:

https://secure-media.collegeboard.org/digitalServices/pdf/professionals/sat-score-use-practices-participating-institutions.pdf

Subject test scores, which must be sent separately, usually do not need to be reported unless specifically required or requested by a college. Additionally, if you re-take a subject test, you are likely not required to send the lower score, unless a college specifically requires it, which is not common. Note that super-scoring does not apply to SAT subject tests, so taking a test more than once will not result in an averaging of the scores.

G. Correct any significant mistakes.

Sometimes, after a submission, a student realizes that a mistake was made somewhere in the application. For example, s/he might review the Common App submission and discover a spelling error, a reference to a specific college in another college's application, or an incorrect grade report. If the student or the guidance counselor believes that this mistake is significant enough that it must be addressed (such as with an incorrect grade report), an email can be sent to admissions with the corrected information and a request that the application be updated.

H. Make other updates.

Both good and bad things happen after submissions that might affect admissions. For example, after submission, a student wins a prestigious award that s/he wants to tell colleges about. Or, a student drops a class that was listed in the mid-year report.

Some colleges have an online portal that allows students to upload pertinent information like this. If not, send an email request to admissions to update the application with the attached information. Note that although some schools do not require mid-year reports, many will accept and consider them.

I. Submit any Honors College/ scholarship applications by their deadlines.

Some colleges automatically consider you for their Honors College or scholarships if your application is completed by a specified deadline. This might be their early action date, their regular deadline date, or some other date. Other colleges require that you complete separate applications for their Honors College and scholarships, so do not to miss out on these opportunities.

J. Submit a FAFSA/CSS/etc. as required.

Many colleges require that you submit a FAFSA, College Board CSS, or their own equivalent financial report before admission, even if you are did not request need-based aid. If you will be relying on a financial package, submit the necessary paperwork as soon as it is permitted, often in October of senior year.

Fafsa information:

https://studentaid.ed.gov/sa/fafsa/filling-out

CSS Profile information:

http://css.collegeboard.org

K. Continue to demonstrate interest.

Don't stop demonstrating interest just because your applications have been submitted. For example: if you haven't visited yet, and get the chance to tour, do it; regularly log in to the college portal; be active on college social media sites.

L. Check that all submissions are complete.

If your high school uses Naviance, check the status of your application on the site. Also confirm via the Common App or college portal that your application is complete. Make sure that all letters of recommendation, transcripts, score reports, and mid-year reports have been received. If anything seems to be missing, check with your guidance office immediately.

M. Keep your grades up.

Don't slack off. Colleges will look at your mid-year and final and consider or reconsider your acceptance based on your performance during senior year.

N. Update your spreadsheet.

Continue to update your spreadsheet as needed.

After Decisions are received:

A. Appeal any deferrals/rejections.

Some students have successfully appealed deferrals and rejections. Sometimes colleges defer or reject applicants by mistake, and a second review reveals their error. Other times, students convince colleges to change their minds.

For example, a college that rejected a student to protect its yield could be swayed by a letter of intent to enroll if admitted. Also, a college might decide to enroll a student who initially applied as a fall applicant but is now willing start early in a summer program, or push the start date off to spring. Sometimes a switch to an "easier" major will yield a different result.

If a college offers an appeal process, follow it. If not, the student or guidance counselor should call admissions and ask for reconsideration. Include in the appeal any updates that might boost chances, and the intent to enroll if admitted. For example:

http://www.huffingtonpost.com/kevin-f-adler/college-decision appeals_b_2918586.html

B. Decide on wait-lists, if necessary.

Wait-lists are not usually an actual numbered "list," but rather a pool of students used to fill openings, usually after the May 1ˢᵗ decision deadline. If you received any college wait-list offers, accept or decline them. You have nothing to lose by adding your name to the list, as long as you have a back-up enrollment at another college, and don't get your hopes up.

While some schools make thousands of offers for only a few openings, other colleges accept a good number of wait-listed applicants. Try to get an idea of the school's past wait-list activity by searching the school's website or the Common Data Set. The CDS reports on Wait-Lists in question C2.

Applicants get chosen from the pool based on what the college class still "needs." If the class lacks students from the south, southern students will get pulled first. Some colleges fill their openings early in the process. Others wait until the last minute, sometimes just days before the semester begins.

If you are offered an acceptance off the wait-list, do not feel obligated to take it.

Oftentimes, you will receive little to no aid, and the least desirable housing and courses. If you do decide to enroll, withdraw your previous enrollment.

C. Weigh your options.

Once you have collected all of your admissions, create a list of pros and cons for each college. Use the categories from Chapter V (Majors, Selectivity, Cost, etc.). Base your decision on realities, and not your "dreams."

D. Attend accepted student day.

If the college offers an accepted student day or weekend, attend. Sometimes they will even reimburse your expenses. Call the Financial Aid office to inquire.

If you cannot attend an accepted student day and have not yet toured the campus, visit. Do not, if at all possible, enroll in a college that you have never seen in person.

E. Appeal your aid package, if necessary.

If you need more aid to attend a college, it never hurts to ask for more help. Visit or call the college financial aid department to let them know that you would love to attend but cannot afford it, and ask them nicely if they can give you any more aid. If you have a written offer from a competing college, ask if they can match it. The worst that they can say is "No."

F. Enroll.

Formally enroll at the college of your choice. Most colleges have an option for you to do on their portal. Screenshot and/or print out your enrollment confirmation.

Do not enroll in more than one college. After the May 1ˢᵗ enrollment deadline, a double-booked student faces rescinded admissions from both colleges. Colleges do find out about these things.

G. Turn down other colleges nicely.

Never burn bridges. If you will not attend a college, let them down nicely. Send an email to admissions telling them that you appreciate their offer, but have decided on a bigger or smaller or closer (etc.) college. Often times, the college will reply with a note holding your offer open for a year. You never know if you might need it.

After enrolling:

A. Submit your enrollment deposit.

The enrollment deposit is usually non-refundable. Meet any deadlines. Screenshot and/or print out your receipt.

B. Submit your housing deposit ASAP.

Although some schools have randomly assigned housing, others' housing placement is on a first-come, first-served basis. It is in your best interest to deposit as early as possible.

Some students enroll and register for housing even if they are not sure that they will attend, if they are worried that the best dorms will fill up early. If you do this and later decide to attend a different college, you must withdraw your enrollment prior to enrolling at a different school. Be prepared to lose at least a portion of the deposit.

C. Meet all minimum requirements before graduating.

Make sure that you are on track to meet all minimum requirements of the college. For example, if the college requires two years of a foreign language, be sure that you will meet that requirement by graduation. If for some reason you will not, look into alternative options, such as summer school.

D. Take all required placement tests.

Some colleges require that you take online placement tests before arriving on campus. Follow all directions very carefully, since you will usually only have one shot at taking the exam. Use the preferred browser and make sure that your Internet connection is strong.

E. Decide on a gap year, if necessary.

Some colleges allow accepted students to defer their admissions for a year or more. If you think that you might wish to take a gap year, check with the college to determine when your decision must be finalized.

F. Fill out college requests.

After enrollment, colleges often send out requests for information. Stay on top of these requests, which might include immunization records, roommate preferences, etc.

G. Consider taking/re-taking SAT IIs for placement or credit.

Some college offer placement or credit for specified SAT II scores. Check the college's practices. Register and take the test(s) during your senior year, if helpful.

H. Send AP/IB/SAT II Scores.

If the college offers placement or credit for specified AP/IB/SAT II scores, and you did not choose to send a free score report when taking the test, pay to send them now.

AP/SAT II:

https://apscore.collegeboard.org/scores/score-reporting//

IB:

http://www.ibo.org/programmes/diploma-programme/assessment-and-exams/requesting-transcripts/

I. Decide on Honors College acceptance, if necessary.

Not everyone who gets admitted to an Honors College within a college chooses to accept. Although many Honors Colleges offer perks like Honors-level courses, early course registration and special dorms, some students decide that they would rather live in the general population and take standard classes. Make the best decision for you.

J. Join "accepted student" social media groups.

You will likely find "(College name) Class of 20xx" Facebook/other social media pages. Some are official, and some are not. Both can be a great way to meet future classmates.

K. Search for a roommate, if possible.

Although many colleges assign roommates randomly, some allow freshman to find their own roommates. Often when they do, the college sets up a portal for students to find each other. Social media is another great tool for this purpose.

L. Register for orientation.

Be on the lookout for information about orientation. Some colleges hold it over the summer, and register students for courses at the same time. If so, it might be best to go to an early session, if possible, since the later sessions may have fewer course options open.

M. Book orientation travel arrangements, if necessary.

As soon as you register for orientation, make your travel arrangements. Sometimes students (and even the parents) stay in the dorms, other times you will need to book a hotel. Space can fill up quickly.

N. Keep on top of communications.

Continue to monitor your college email address. Login occasionally to the portal to make sure that you are not missing any important information. Reply promptly to any requests.

O. Sign required documents if under 18.

If you will be under 18 when the semester begins, there might be special paperwork from the college that you and your parent will need to sign.

P. Obtain other paperwork if over 18.

If you will be over 18, consider obtaining a health care proxy and a durable power of attorney. Without these, your parents may not be able to receive any medial information, make medial decisions, or handle money matters for you if necessary. You can visit an attorney to draw these up, or do it yourself for free on sites such as:

http://www.caringinfo.org/i4a/pages/index.cfm?pageid=3289

https://powerofattorney.com/durable/

Q. Waive health insurance, if applicable.

If you or your parents have health insurance, you might be able to save money by waiving the campus health insurance. Make sure that if you do so, you will still be able visit the campus health center when needed. Some colleges require that you to make this waiver every semester.

R. Consider attending any summer activities hosted by the college.

Some colleges offer social events for students before the semester begins. It could be something as simple as a bar-b-q, or as extravagant as a weeklong outdoor camping adventure. These are great opportunities to get acquainted, so take them, if possible.

S. Learn how to do laundry/bank/other things for yourself.

If you have never really had to fend for yourself, now is the time to start. You need to learn, in the very least, to clean up after yourself, do your laundry, make a withdrawal from the bank, and fill a prescription. The more you do now, the easier your transition to college will be.

T. Start a convenient bank account.

Once you learn how to use an ATM, start an account with a bank that is located on or very near campus. Search what banks are accessible to students within walking distance, and then visit a local or online branch to open a fee-free student account with an accompanying free ATM card.

U. Pack.

You will find lists of what you should pack for college all over the Internet. Less is more; do not buy tons of things that you might not need and can have shipped later, if necessary. Your storage space will likely be limited in a dorm, and Amazon Student Prime is your friend.

The most important things that you will need are any prescriptions/medicines, a locked box to keep them in, and your ID, which includes your Social Security card if you will be seeking employment.

V. Make move-in arrangements ASAP.

Determine how you will get yourself and your belongings to college for move-in. Check the college calendar for move-in dates. Make any necessary arrangements.

W. Book parent weekend travel arrangements ASAP.

As soon as you obtain the dates for parent weekend, make travel arrangements. Hotels fill up quickly. Purchase tickets for any sporting events or activities that interest you.

X. Book remaining travel arrangements.

Flights and trains can cost a fortune and/or fill up if you wait too long to book.

Check the college calendar for fall, Thanksgiving, winter and spring break dates; look at class syllabuses to determine if classes will be held or cancelled on the day before or after break. Make all necessary arrangements as soon as possible.

Appendix 2

Sample Spreadsheet

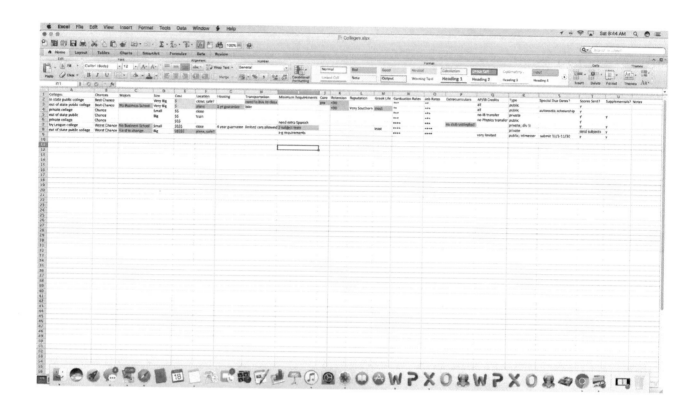

About the Author:

Dawn Schildhorn is an Attorney licensed to practice law in multiple states. After having children, she left a successful legal career to become a stay-at-home mom.

When her kids entered highly competitive high schools, she realized that great grades and standardized test scores were not enough to get them admitted to selective colleges. So, she used her training as a prosecutor to prove, beyond a reasonable doubt, what it would take to weigh the odds in their favor.

After conducting extensive and exhausting research, Dawn identified the 12 things that matter most in the college admission process, and formulated corresponding steps for getting admitted.

She used this information to help her own high school students, and many others over the past six years, reach their seemingly impossible goals of getting accepted to Ivy League and other selective colleges, some with generous scholarships. This book reveals her "secrets" to tipping the scale in your favor and getting admitted.

Dawn is now enjoying her third career as the highly respected private college counselor known as "The Ivy Counselor." Visit www.TheIvyCounselor.com for more information.

This book is dedicated to all of the high school students who work so hard to get admitted to college. You amaze me every single day!
And, especially to my own children and my husband, for making me a mom. I would not be me without you.

52792690R00060

Made in the USA
San Bernardino, CA
28 August 2017